PREFACE

1. Scope

This publication provides doctrine for planning and executing peace operations.

2. Purpose

This publication has been prepared under the direction of the Chairman of the Joint Chiefs of Staff. It sets forth joint doctrine to govern the activities and performance of the Armed Forces of the United States in joint operations and provides the doctrinal basis for interagency coordination and for US military involvement in multinational operations. It provides military guidance for the exercise of authority by combatant commanders and other joint force commanders (JFCs) and prescribes joint doctrine for operations, education, and training. It provides military guidance for use by the Armed Forces in preparing their appropriate plans. It is not the intent of this publication to restrict the authority of the JFC from organizing the force and executing the mission in a manner the JFC deems most appropriate to ensure unity of effort in the accomplishment of the overall objective.

3. Application

a. Joint doctrine established in this publication applies to the Joint Staff, commanders of combatant commands, subunified commands, joint task forces, subordinate components of these commands, and the Services.

b. The guidance in this publication is authoritative; as such, this doctrine will be followed except when, in the judgment of the commander, exceptional circumstances dictate otherwise. If conflicts arise between the contents of this publication and the contents of Service publications, this publication will take precedence unless the Chairman of the Joint Chiefs of Staff, normally in coordination with the other members of the Joint Chiefs of Staff, has provided more current and specific guidance. Commanders of forces operating as part of a multinational (alliance or coalition) military command should follow multinational doctrine and procedures ratified by the United States. For doctrine and procedures not ratified by the United States, commanders should evaluate and follow the multinational command's doctrine and procedures, where applicable and consistent with US law, regulations, and doctrine.

For the Chairman of the Joint Chiefs of Staff:

WALTER L. SHARP
Lieutenant General, USA
Director, Joint Staff

Intentionally Blank

SUMMARY OF CHANGES
REVISION OF JOINT PUBLICATION 3-07.3
DATED 12 FEBRUARY 1999

- **Places peace operations (PO) as crisis response and limited contingency operations in the new range of military operations**

- **Expands the definition of PO to include peacekeeping operations, military peace enforcement operations, peace building post-conflict actions, peacemaking processes, and conflict prevention**

- **Discusses the 15 fundamentals of PO**

- **Adds transition planning and risk of mission creep to the coverage of the PO environment and characteristics**

- **Adds the campaign plan to the key documents in PO**

- **Revises the fundamentals of peacekeeping operations**

- **Updates the listing of maritime forces support capabilities in peacekeeping operations**

- **Revises peacekeeping tasks**

- **Expands the discussion of the description of peace enforcement operations**

- **Revises the fundamentals of peace enforcement operations**

- **Revises peace enforcement tasks**

- **Greatly expands the discussion of planning considerations for peace enforcement operations**

- **Updates coverage of peace enforcement operations employment phases**

- **Adds a chapter discussing peace building; adds post-conflict actions**

- **Updates appendix on key documents in PO**

- **Adds several new figures illustrating command relationships in PO**

- **Adds definition for the term "conflict prevention"**

- **Modifies the definitions of "peace operations" and "preventive deployment"**

Intentionally Blank

TABLE OF CONTENTS

APPENDIX

GLOSSARY

FIGURE

EXECUTIVE SUMMARY
COMMANDER'S OVERVIEW

- **Provides Primer for Peace Operations**

- **Covers Peacekeeping Operations**

- **Discusses Peace Enforcement Operations**

- **Covers Peace Building**

Overview

As with other types of military operations, the character of peace operations will be unique, reflecting the political, military, economic, social, information, and infrastructure characteristics of the environment.

For the Armed Forces of the United States, peace operations (PO) are crisis response and limited contingency operations, and normally include international efforts and military missions to contain conflict, redress the peace, and shape the environment to support reconciliation and rebuilding and to facilitate the transition to legitimate governance. PO include peacekeeping operations (PKO), peace building (PB) post-conflict actions, peacemaking (PM) processes, conflict prevention, and military peace enforcement operations (PEO). PO may be conducted under the sponsorship of the United Nations (UN), another intergovernmental organization (IGO), within a coalition of agreeing nations, or unilaterally.

Fundamentals of Peace Operations

Fifteen fundamentals apply to peace operations (PO).

The **15 fundamentals of PO** are discussed below.

Consent. In PO, the level of consent determines the fundamentals. There may be consent at the strategic level among the party representatives signing an agreement. However, renegade local groups at the tactical level may disagree with their leaders and remain hostile to PO. By its nature, a PO force capable of conducting PEO must be employed in PO when there is no general consent or when there is uncertainty regarding consent.

Impartiality. Impartiality distinguishes PO from other operations. Impartiality requires the PO force to act on behalf of the peace process and mandate, and not show preference for any faction or group over another. This fundamental applies to the belligerents or parties to the dispute, not to possible spoilers (e.g., terrorists, criminals, or other hostile elements outside the peace process).

The PO force maintains impartiality by focusing on the current behavior of the involved parties — employing force (i.e., PEO) because of what is being done, not because of who is doing it.

Transparency. The PO forces must make the parties and the populace aware of the operational mandate, mission, intentions, and techniques used to ensure compliance. Transparency serves to reinforce legitimacy and impartiality.

Credibility. Credibility is essential to ensure mission accomplishment. Credibility reflects the belligerents' assessment of the capability of the PO force to accomplish its mission.

Freedom of Movement. Freedom of movement equates to maintaining the initiative. As amplified in the mandate, no restrictions are allowed against the movement of the PO force. Freedom of movement for the civilian population may be a necessary condition to maintain consent and allow the transition to peace to continue.

Flexibility and Adaptability. The complex multinational and interagency environment in which the PO force operates require commanders at all levels to place a premium on initiative and flexibility. Commanders and staffs must continually analyze their mission in the changing political context, and change tasks, missions, and operations as appropriate.

Civil-Military Harmonization and Cooperation. Civil-military harmonization and cooperation is a central feature of PO that enhances the credibility of the PO force, promotes consent and legitimacy, and encourages the parties to the conflict to work toward a peaceful settlement, thereby facilitating the transition to civil control.

Restraint and Minimum Force. The PO force must apply military force prudently, judiciously, and with discipline. A single act could cause significant military and political consequences. Restraint requires the careful and disciplined balancing of the need for security, achievement of military objectives, and attainment of the end state.

Objective/End State. Direct every PO towards clearly defined, decisive, and achievable objectives and the desired end state. The PO force commander should translate the strategic guidance into appropriate objectives through rigorous and continuous mission analyses.

Perseverance. Nations involved in PO must prepare for the measured, protracted employment of the joint force and its capabilities in support of the PO mandate and directive. Some PO may require years to achieve desired results.

Unity of Effort. Unity of effort emphasizes the need for ensuring that all means are directed to a common purpose. In PO, achieving unity of effort is often complicated by a variety of international, foreign, and domestic military and nonmilitary participants, the lack of definitive command arrangements, and varying views of the objective.

Legitimacy. In PO, legitimacy is perceived by interested audiences as the legality, morality, or fairness of a set of actions. Such audiences may include the US public, foreign nations, civil populations in the operational area, and the participating forces. If a PO is perceived as legitimate by both the citizens of the nations contributing the forces and the citizens of the country being entered, the PO will have a better chance of long-term success.

Security. The PO force may be given specific responsibilities for the protection of civilian components of the operation. If security of resources and mission capability is compromised, this can affect the ultimate success of PO.

Mutual Respect and Cultural Awareness. Developing mutual respect, rapport, and cultural awareness among multinational partners takes time, patience, and the concerted efforts of leaders at all levels of command.

Current and Sufficient Intelligence. The intelligence requirements in support of PO are similar in nature, but may be much larger (by volume), to those required during major operations. Intelligence provides assessments that help the joint force commander (JFC) decide which forces to deploy; when, how, and where to deploy them; and how to employ them in a manner that accomplishes the mission.

Types of Peace Operations

PO are crisis response and limited contingency operations conducted by a combination of military forces and nonmilitary organizations. They include five types.

Peacekeeping Operations. PKO consist of military operations undertaken with the consent of all major parties to a dispute, and are designed to monitor and facilitate implementation of an agreement to support diplomatic efforts to reach a long-term political settlement. Before PKO begin, a credible truce or cease fire must be in effect and the parties to the dispute must consent to the operation. PKO take place following diplomatic negotiation and agreement among the parties to a dispute, the sponsoring organization, and the potential troop-contributing nations.

Peace Enforcement Operations. PEO are generally coercive in nature and rely on the threat of or use of force; however, PEO may also be co-optive in nature, relying on the development of working relationships with locals. PEO may include the enforcement of sanctions and exclusion zones, protection of personnel conducting foreign humanitarian assistance missions, restoration of order, and forcible separation of belligerent parties or parties to a dispute. However, the impartiality with which the PO force treats all parties and the nature of its objectives separates PEO from major combat operations.

Peace Building. PB covers **post-conflict actions,** predominantly diplomatic, economic, legal, and security related, that support political, social, and military measures aimed at strengthening political settlements and legitimate governance and rebuilding governmental infrastructure and institutions. PB begins while PEO or PKO are underway and may continue for years.

Peacemaking. PM is a diplomatic process aimed at establishing a cease fire or an otherwise peaceful settlement of a conflict. For the PO force commander, PM is the least understood term. It is misunderstood primarily because it is not military-led. Military support to PM includes provision of military expertise to the PM process, military-to-military relations, security assistance, peacetime deployments or other activities that influence the disputing parties to seek a diplomatic settlement.

Conflict Prevention. Conflict prevention consists of diplomatic and other actions taken in advance of a predictable crisis to prevent or limit violence, deter parties, and reach an agreement short of conflict. Military activities will be tailored to meet the political and situational demands, but will generally fall within the following categories: early warning, surveillance, training and security sector reform, preventative deployment, and sanctions and embargoes.

Command and Control for Peace Operation

The United States may participate in PO under various command authority arrangements.

In any of these arrangements, US forces will report to the US chain of command. However, in multinational PO, US forces may also report to the sponsoring IGO such as the UN, North Atlantic Treaty Organization, Organization of African Unity, Organization of American States, or European Union. By law, the President retains command authority over US forces. However, as Commander in Chief, the President has the authority to place US forces under the operational control (OPCON) of a foreign commander when doing so serves American security interests. The greater the anticipated US military role, the less likely it will be that the US will agree to have a non-US commander exercise OPCON over US forces. Any large scale participation of US forces in a PEO that is likely to involve combat will ordinarily be conducted under US command authority.

Although in certain circumstances US forces may be placed under the OPCON of non-US commanders, the US chain of command will remain inviolate, running from the President to the supported JFC.

CONCLUSION

This publication provides doctrine for planning and executing peace operations.

Intentionally Blank

CHAPTER I
PRIMER FOR PEACE OPERATIONS

"The United States will stand with and support advocates of freedom in every land. Though our principles are consistent, our tactics will vary. They will reflect, in part, where each government is on the path from tyranny to democracy. In some cases, we will take vocal and visible steps on behalf of immediate change. In other cases, we will lend more quiet support to lay the foundation for future reforms. As we consider which approaches to take, we will be guided by what will most effectively advance freedom's cause while we balance other interests that are also vital to the security and well-being of the American people."

**National Security Strategy of the
United States of America
March 2006**

1. Introduction

a. Joint doctrine addresses a broad range of military operations, including crisis response and limited contingency operations. Peace operations (PO) are a type of joint operation (called peace support operations [PSO] in the North Atlantic Treaty Organization [NATO] alliance). **In this joint publication (JP), for clarity, the US terms are used except where specifically noted as "United Nations (UN) peacekeeping" or "UN peacekeepers."**

b. Common to most military doctrine is the recognition that peace is a product of healthy societies' ability to settle disagreements without resulting to force. Once an armed conflict begins, the will of parties involved influences the instruments of national and international power (i.e., diplomatic, informational, military, and economic). NATO doctrine for PSO includes humanitarian efforts as part of allied joint doctrine, while US joint doctrine for PO does not. US doctrine addresses such efforts separately, but in a manner that closely links those humanitarian efforts with the conduct of PO.

c. For the Armed Forces of the United States, PO are crisis response and limited contingency operations, and normally include international efforts and military missions to contain conflict, redress the peace, and shape the environment to support reconciliation and rebuilding and to facilitate the transition to legitimate governance. PO include peacekeeping operations (PKO), peace building (PB) post-conflict actions, peacemaking (PM) processes, conflict prevention, and military peace enforcement operations (PEO). PO may be conducted under the sponsorship of the UN, another intergovernmental organization (IGO), within a coalition of agreeing nations, or unilaterally.

d. As with other types of military operations, the character of PO will be unique, reflecting the political, military, economic, social, information, and infrastructure characteristics of the environment.

2. Legal Basis of Peace Operations

a. While the United States may conduct PO independently, normally PO will be conducted under the sponsorship of the UN or another IGO.

b. The UN Charter provides several means for the international community to address threats to peace and security. Although the terms "peacekeeping" and "peace enforcement" are not in the UN Charter, they generally describe actions taken under the Charter's Chapter VI, "Pacific Settlement of Disputes," Chapter VII, "Action with Respect to Threats to the Peace, Breaches of the Peace, and Acts of Aggression," and Chapter VIII, "Regional Arrangements," respectively. Chapter VI of the UN Charter addresses peaceful means of establishing or maintaining peace through conciliation, mediation, adjudication, and diplomacy, while Chapter VII provides the UN Security Council (UNSC) with a wide range of enforcement actions — from diplomatic and economic measures to the extensive application of armed force by the air, land, and maritime forces of member nations.

c. Under Chapter VIII of the UN Charter, regional organizations such as NATO, the Organization of American States (OAS), the Organization of African Unity (OAU), the Economic Community of West African States, and the European Union (EU) may also act to prevent, halt, or contain conflict in their respective regions.

d. Similarly, some nations have negotiated **multilateral agreements to create PO** independent of any permanent international forum. However, such operations have usually taken place with the tacit approval of a regional organization or the UN.

3. Fundamentals of Peace Operations

There are certain **fundamentals that apply specifically to PO**, although not all are necessary for success in every PO. They are, rather, general principles which should hold true for most POs. The **15 fundamentals of PO** are depicted in Figure I-1 and discussed below.

a. **Consent.** In major operations and campaigns, consent is not an issue, but in PO, the level of consent determines the fundamentals. One side may consent in whole or in part; multiple parties may consent; there may be no consent; or the consent may vary dramatically over time. There may be consent at the strategic level among the party representatives signing an agreement. However, renegade local groups at the tactical level may disagree with their leaders and remain hostile to PO. By its nature, a PO force capable of conducting PEO must be employed in PO when there is no general consent or when there is uncertainty regarding consent. Figure I-2 shows the relationship between the level of consent and PO force capability requirements for operations. When strong consent or commitment by the parties to the peace agreement exists, a reduced military force capability is possible. Note that degrees or levels of consent can change over time. The objective of the PO force is to increase the consent for the peace process by gaining broad and deep buy-in to the mandate, peace agreement, or the plan for governance. As consent becomes more general, the PO force can reduce its force capability. As the level of consent decreases, the level of force capability to enforce compliance must increase, creating

FUNDAMENTALS OF PEACE OPERATIONS

Consent
Impartiality
Transparency
Credibility
Freedom of Movement
Flexibility and Adaptability
Civil-Military Harmonization and Cooperation
Restraint and Minimum Force
Objective/End State
Perseverance
Unity of Effort
Legitimacy
Security
Mutual Respect and Cultural Awareness
Current and Sufficient Intelligence

Figure I-1. Fundamentals of Peace Operations

conditions for PEO. **The promotion of consent** is fundamental to achieving the national end state in all PO. Closely linked to consent is **compliance** with the agreement or mandate. The enforcement of compliance may be a necessary condition to gain or maintain consent. Actions by PO forces during PO can build or destroy consent. Joint force commanders (JFCs) should seek ways to promote consent by giving the people, parties, and local institutions a stake in the peace process. Joint military commissions, liaison officers (LNOs), media broadcasts, and leaders throughout the PO force are key means to promote consent and share agreements. If consent is lost during PO, the assigned PO force may no longer be capable of dealing with the situation. New political decisions, mandates, rules of engagement (ROE), or force compositions will be necessary. Additional capabilities and resources may be required or the joint force may need to be withdrawn.

b. **Impartiality** distinguishes PO from other operations. Impartiality requires the PO force to act on behalf of the peace process and mandate, and not show preference for any faction or group over another. This fundamental applies to the belligerents or parties to the dispute, not to possible spoilers (e.g., terrorists, criminals, or other hostile elements outside the peace process). The PO force maintains impartiality by focusing on the current behavior of the involved parties — employing force (i.e., PEO) because of what is being done, not because of who is doing it. The degree to which the PO force acts in an impartial manner and the degree to which the belligerent parties perceive the PO force to be impartial, combine to influence the PO. Impartiality should not be confused with neutrality. Impartiality does not imply that PO will affect all sides

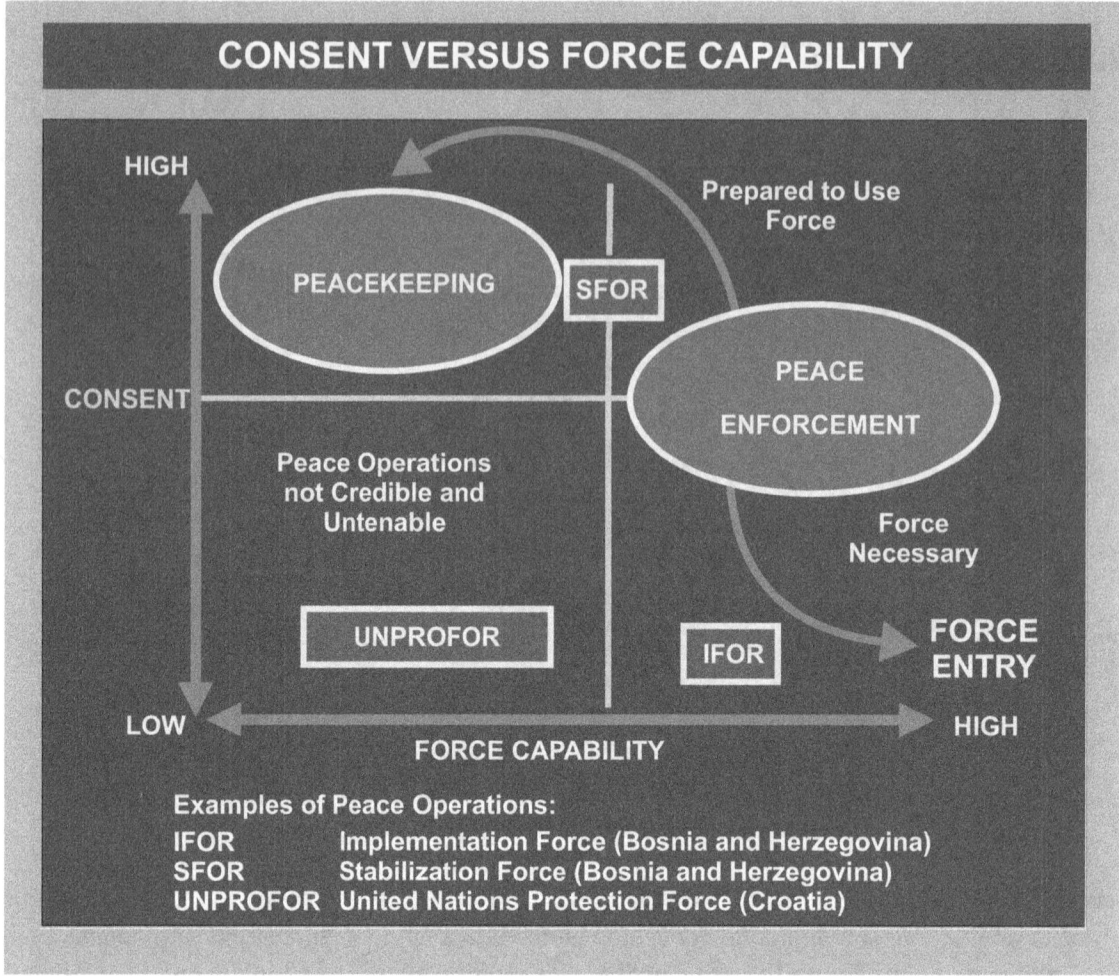

Figure I-2. Consent Versus Force Capability

equally. Impartiality does not preclude the use of force in any PO. In PKO use of force is for self-defense; in PEO use of force is used to compel or coerce compliance with established rules.

c. **Transparency.** The PO forces must make the parties and the populace aware of the operational mandate, mission, intentions, and techniques used to ensure compliance. Transparency serves to reinforce legitimacy and impartiality. A failure to communicate will foster suspicion and may erode the development of the trust and confidence on which the long-term success of the operation depends. Integrated and synchronized information operations (IO) can facilitate transparency. Civil-military harmonization, joint commissions, and an effective liaison system reinforce transparency. JFCs must balance the need for transparency against the need for operations security.

d. **Credibility** is essential to ensure mission accomplishment. Credibility reflects the belligerents' assessment of the capability of the PO force to accomplish its mission. It must discharge its duties swiftly and firmly, leaving no doubt as to its capabilities and commitment. All personnel must consistently demonstrate the highest standards of discipline, control, and professional behavior on and off duty.

e. **Freedom of Movement** equates to maintaining the initiative. As amplified in the mandate, no restrictions should be allowed against the movement of the PO force. Freedom of movement for the civilian population may be a necessary condition to maintain consent and allow the transition to peace to continue. If the belligerents persist in denying freedom of movement, the authorizing political organization must assess the situation to determine if the mandate must change or the force must withdraw.

f. **Flexibility and Adaptability.** The complex multinational and interagency environment in which the PO force operates requires commanders at all levels to place a premium on initiative and flexibility. Commanders and staffs must continually analyze their mission in the changing political context, and change tasks, missions, and operations as appropriate. The successful transition to peace involves managing change. Forces should be able to adapt and move from one activity to another on short notice.

g. **Civil-Military Harmonization and Cooperation** is a central feature of PO that enhances the credibility of the PO force, promotes consent and legitimacy, and encourages the parties to the conflict to work toward a peaceful settlement, thereby facilitating the transition to civil control. Civil-military harmonization and cooperation includes those civil-military operations (CMO) that promote the coordination, integration, and synchronization of civil and military efforts and actions to build the peace. At the operational level, commanders should coordinate the use of joint military and joint civil commissions ensuring that all stakeholders are represented. At the tactical level, the timely and effective harmonization, cooperation, and coordination of PO forces with those of civilian agencies is essential for mission success. Cooperation should be supported by establishment of committees, action groups, and robust liaison with agencies and organizations involved in the operational area, and respect for their roles and missions. To assist in this cooperation and coordination of activities, commanders may create a civil-military operations center (CMOC) or a civil-military cooperation (CIMIC) center.

h. **Restraint and Minimum Force.** Apply military force prudently, judiciously, and with discipline. A single act could cause significant military and political consequences. Restraint requires the careful and disciplined balancing of the need for security, achievement of military objectives, and attainment of the end state. The use of excessive force could antagonize the parties involved, thereby damaging the legitimacy of the organization that uses it while potentially enhancing the legitimacy of the opposing party. Commanders at all levels must take proactive steps to ensure their personnel are properly trained. ROE in PO are generally restrictive, detailed, and sensitive to political and cultural concerns. Since the domestic law of some nations may be more restrictive concerning the use of force than permitted under coalition or allied force ROE, commanders must be aware of national restrictions. The use of nonlethal weapons must be considered an additional option to force commanders.

i. **Objective/End State.** Direct every PO towards clearly defined, decisive, and achievable objectives and the desired end state. The PO force commander should translate the strategic guidance into appropriate objectives through rigorous and continuous mission analyses. The JFC should carefully explain to political authorities the implications of political decisions on capabilities and risk to military forces. Care should be taken to avoid misunderstandings stemming from a lack of common terminology.

j. **Perseverance.** Prepare for the measured, protracted employment of the joint force and its capabilities in support of the PO mandate and directive. Some PO may require years to achieve desired results. It is important to **assess possible responses to a crisis** in terms of each option's impact on the achievement of the long-term political objectives. This will often involve diplomatic, informational, and economic measures to supplement and complement military efforts.

k. **Unity of Effort.** Unity of effort emphasizes the need for ensuring that all means are directed to a common purpose. In PO, achieving unity of effort is often complicated by a variety of international, foreign, and domestic military and nonmilitary participants, the lack of definitive command arrangements, and varying views of the objective. While the chain of command for US military forces remains inviolate, command arrangements among multinational partners may be less well-defined and may not include full command authority. PO force commanders may answer to a civilian chief, such as an ambassador, or may themselves employ the resources of a civilian organization. Additionally, unity of effort among the various nations' militaries involved in the PO can be greatly enhanced using time proven cooperative models such as the Multinational Planning Augmentation Team, Multinational Force (MNF) Standing Operating Procedures (SOPs), and Multinational Coordination Centers as part of the coalition task force headquarters. These models are not based on command and control; rather they are based on clearly articulated cooperative processes that enhance coordination and unity of effort overall (refer to JP 3-16, *Multinational Operations*, for a full outline.)

l. **Legitimacy.** In PO, legitimacy is perceived by interested audiences as the legality, morality, or fairness of a set of actions. Such audiences may include the US public, foreign nations, civil populations in the operational area, and the participating forces. If a PO is perceived as legitimate by both the citizens of the nations contributing the forces and the citizens of the country being entered, the PO will have a better chance of long-term success. Restricting the use of force, restructuring the type of forces employed, and ensuring the disciplined conduct of the forces involved may reinforce legitimacy. The perception of legitimacy by the US public is strengthened if there are obvious national or humanitarian interests at stake. Another aspect of this principle is the legitimacy bestowed upon a local government through the perception of the populace that it governs. During operations in an area where a government does not exist, extreme caution should be used to avoid inadvertently legitimizing nonrecognized factions.

m. **Security.** The PO force may be given specific responsibilities for the protection of civilian components of the operation. If security of resources and mission capability is compromised, this can affect the ultimate success of PO. The ability to establish and maintain security complements the PO principle of credibility.

n. **Mutual Respect and Cultural Awareness.** Developing mutual respect, rapport, and cultural awareness among multinational partners takes time, patience, and the concerted efforts of leaders at all levels of command. Key ingredients for success in the multinational environment include clear and common understanding, mutual respect, and common goals among supporting allies. Equally challenging is the professional conduct and how the PO force treats the local population with respect to their cultures, languages, and customs.

o. **Current and Sufficient Intelligence.** The intelligence requirements in support of PO are similar in nature, but may be much larger (by volume), to those required during major operations. Intelligence provides assessments that help the JFC decide which forces to deploy; when, how, and where to deploy them; and how to employ them in a manner that accomplishes the mission. Intelligence is essential to force protection. Intelligence efforts must simultaneously support PKO while providing the JFC with indications and warnings of any possible escalation of violence.

4. Types of Peace Operations

PO includes the five types of operations depicted in Figure I-3. The nature of the crisis will determine the level and type of response. It is possible for multiple types of PO to occur simultaneously within an AOR. The military objective in these operations is to create the conditions for other diplomatic, economic, and humanitarian activities to achieve the political objective stated in the mandate and to transition from involvement. Optimally, PO forces should be able to transition from one type of PO to another, though in some circumstances, the PO force may have to be replaced with another PO force under a different mandate during this transition. PB creates a self-sustaining peace and avoids a relapse into conflict. PKO and PEO are designed to establish a stable environment in which PB can occur. Although not in the lead, the military provides necessary support to ensure PM and conflict prevention succeed; however, because PM and conflict prevention are primarily diplomatic efforts, they are not afforded full chapters in this publication.

a. **Peacekeeping Operations.** PKO consist of military operations undertaken with the consent of all major parties to a dispute, and are designed to monitor and facilitate implementation of an agreement to support diplomatic efforts to reach a long-term political settlement. Before PKO begin, a credible truce or cease fire must be in effect, and the parties to the dispute must **consent** to the operation. PKO take place following diplomatic negotiation and agreement among the parties to a dispute, the sponsoring organization, and the potential troop-contributing nations. The UN Charter makes no specific mention of PKO, per se. PKO seek to settle disputes through the medium of peaceful third-party initiatives. PKO have usually been conducted in accordance with Chapter VI of the UN Charter. Using force in a PKO is generally limited to self-defense. A loss of consent by the parties usually necessitates the withdrawal of the PO force or a change in its mission to PEO.

See Chapter II, "Peacekeeping Operations."

b. **Peace Enforcement Operations**

(1) PEO are generally coercive in nature and rely on the threat or use of force; however, PEO may also be co-optive in nature, relying on the development of working relationships with locals. **PEO** may include the enforcement of sanctions and exclusion zones, protection of

TYPES OF PEACE OPERATIONS

PEACEKEEPING

Military operations undertaken with the consent of all major parties to a dispute, designed to monitor and facilitate implementation of an agreement (cease fire, truce, or other such agreement) and support diplomatic efforts to reach a long-term political settlement.

PEACE ENFORCEMENT

Application of military force, or the threat of its use, normally pursuant to international authorization, to compel compliance with resolutions or sanctions designed to maintain or restore peace and order.

PEACE BUILDING

Stability actions, predominately diplomatic and economic, that strengthen and rebuild governmental infrastructure and institutions in order to avoid a relapse into conflict.

PEACEMAKING

The process of diplomacy, mediation, negotiation, or other forms of peaceful settlements that arranges an end to a dispute and resolves issues that led to it.

CONFLICT PREVENTION

A peace operation employing complementary diplomatic, civil, and, when necessary, military means, to monitor and identify the causes of conflict, and take timely action to prevent the occurrence, escalation, or resumption of hostilities. Activities aimed at conflict prevention are often conducted under Chapter VI of the United Nations Charter. Conflict prevention can include fact-finding missions, consultations, warnings, inspections, and monitoring.

Note: Only peacekeeping, peace enforcement, and peace building are discussed in detailed chapters. Peacemaking and conflict prevention are primarily diplomatic efforts supported by the military thus are not afforded full chapters in this publication.

Figure I-3. Types of Peace Operations

personnel conducting foreign humanitarian assistance (FHA) missions, restoration of order, and forcible separation of belligerent parties or parties to a dispute. However, the impartiality with which the PO force treats all parties and the nature of its objectives separates PEO from major operations. Should it be necessary to conduct operations in support of one particular party against another, impartiality would be lost and PEO would deteriorate. If this situation develops, then the authorizing authority must reassess the PO. The purpose of PEO is not to destroy or defeat an adversary, but to use force or threat of force to establish a safe and secure environment so that PB can succeed. The term "peace enforcement" is not specifically mentioned in the UN Charter; however, the UN Charter's language allows the UNSC to authorize military operations 'as may be necessary to restore or maintain international peace and security.'

(2) PEO are often conducted by lead regional organizations or a coalition of states under a lead nation. Since PEO may include offensive and defensive operations, missions must be clear and end states defined. In a particular operational area, offensive, defensive, and stability operations may occur simultaneously. Due to the nature of PO, civilian considerations are key.

See Chapter III, "Peace Enforcement Operations."

c. **Peace Building.** PB covers **post-conflict actions,** predominantly diplomatic, economic, legal, and security related, that support political, social, and military measures aimed at strengthening political settlements and legitimate governance and rebuilding governmental infrastructure and institutions. PB begins while PEO or PKO are underway and may continue for years. Military support to PB may include PKO, nation assistance, or other activities that establish an environment conducive to continuing the post-conflict political process.

See Chapter IV, "Peace Building."

d. **Peacemaking**

(1) PM is a diplomatic process aimed at establishing a cease fire or an otherwise peaceful settlement of a conflict.

(2) For the PO force commander, PM is the least understood term. It is misunderstood primarily because it is not military-led. In US joint doctrine, PM tools include negotiation, inquiry, mediation, conciliation, arbitration, judicial settlement, resort to regional agencies or arrangements, or other peaceful means. PM is predominantly diplomatic efforts but may be supported by a PO force. Operations in support of PM efforts should not be referred to as "peacemaking operations."

(3) The military does not have the lead, but military leaders are normally involved in negotiating the military aspects of a peace agreement. This often includes face-to-face meetings with the leaders of the warring factions.

(4) Military support to PM includes provision of military expertise to the PM process, military-to-military relations, security assistance, peacetime deployments, or other activities that influence the disputing parties to seek a diplomatic settlement.

e. **Conflict Prevention.** Conflict prevention consists of diplomatic and other actions taken in advance of a predictable crisis to prevent or limit violence, deter parties, and reach an agreement short of conflict. Military activities will be tailored to meet the political and situational demands, but will generally fall within the following categories: early warning, surveillance, training and security sector reform, preventative deployment, and sanctions and embargoes.

5. The Peace Operations Environment and Characteristics

a. **Primacy of Political Objectives and Political Limitations.** In both PO and in major operations, political objectives and political constraints are derived from the national security strategy, national defense strategy, national military strategy, and US Government (USG) policy. Military personnel at all levels should understand the objectives of the operation and the potential impact of inappropriate military actions. Having such an understanding helps avoid actions that may have adverse effects on the force or the mission at the tactical or operational level, and catastrophic effects on USG policy at the strategic level.

b. **Complexity, Ambiguity, and Uncertainty.** PO often take place in political, military, and cultural situations that are highly fluid and dynamic. Ambiguity may be caused by unresolved political issues, an unclear description or misunderstanding of a desired end state, or difficulty in gaining international consensus. Additionally, the deploying PO forces may have little or no familiarity with the operational area or the complex ethnic and cultural issues that, in some cases, led to the dispute.

c. **Parties to the Dispute.** The parties to the dispute, also called belligerents, may or may not have professional armies or organized groups responding reliably to a chain of command. PO may take place within a functioning state or within a failing or failed state. Rogue, undisciplined elements or paramilitary units may be present. Decisions by the leaders may not bind the subordinate elements. Local leaders may authorize splinter groups to continue to conduct operations while allowing themselves a degree of deniability. Loosely organized groups of irregulars, criminal syndicates, or other hostile elements of the population may be present. The PO force should focus on those elements that seek to spoil the peace process. These "spoilers," whether internal or external, to a peace process, are agents, organizations, or factions that threaten the success of the PO. They willfully obstruct US and multinational strategic or operational objectives. Spoilers can be individuals, organizations, or governments. Each type of spoiler requires a different strategy to eliminate, contain, or satisfy them. Regardless of the approach, the PO force commander must identify and understand the underlying issues motivating each spoiler.

d. **The Planning Process.** The PO planning process is the same as for any other military operation. Commanders and their staffs need to ensure they have a complete understanding of the specified and implied tasks and the end state before planning begins.

For further planning guidance, refer to JP 5-0, Joint Operation Planning, *and JP 3-33,* Joint Task Force Headquarters.

(1) **Location of Operations.** Frequently, PO will take place in both austere and highly populated urban environments. Logistics may become a major challenge when PO are conducted in remote areas with poor air and sea ports, over rugged and broad spans of terrain with poor transportation networks, or in cities with underdeveloped infrastructure. Therefore, deploying forces requires careful time-phasing with the appropriate resources to accomplish the mission and compensate for shortfalls. Carefully planned and executed reconnaissance surveys of anticipated operational areas are essential.

(2) **Duration of Operations.** PO may be conducted on short notice or evolve over a period of time, and may require long-term commitments to resolve the issues that led to the escalation of tension or conflict. However, PO can help establish stable and secure conditions for progress towards long-term political settlements. Time constraints for the duration of the operation are high-level politico-military decisions. On the one hand, the declaration of an operational timescale can cede the initiative to the parties to the conflict. They can then wait out the departure of the PO force. They can harden their positions or present a false front. On the other hand, **establishing a fixed date for the participation of the PO force** serves notice that parties must also work diligently to resolve their differences, unless they are willing to forgo the support of the PO force. In either case, establishing the conditions which define attainment of the military end state and directing efforts to create those conditions is important.

(3) **Geospatial intelligence** (GEOINT) is the exploitation and analysis of imagery and geospatial information to describe, assess, and visually depict physical features and geographically referenced activities on the Earth. GEOINT consists of imagery, imagery intelligence, and geospatial information. The National Geospatial-Intelligence Agency (NGA) should be engaged early in the PO planning processes and throughout the operation, via the NGA support team.

e. **Force Structure and Composition.** Close politico-military communication is essential to assure the composition of the PO force is based on the mission, the threat, and possible no-notice operational permutations. PO force composition should be robust enough to respond to threats to force security. A force cap may establish limits on the number of military personnel, number and type of weapons, or the type of units to be deployed in support of PO.

f. **Interagency Coordination.** In PO, other US agencies including the Department of State (DOS) will be involved. Therefore, commanders should ensure military activities are closely coordinated and when appropriate integrated with the activities of other agencies to optimize the effectiveness of the total effort. The Ambassador is responsible for all USG elements in country except those under the authority of the combatant commander (CCDR). Therefore, close coordination with the Ambassador's Country Team is essential. Emphasis should be placed on early establishment of liaison with the Country Team and among the various agencies operating in country. At the geographic combatant commander (GCC) level, a Joint Interagency Coordination Group offers regular, timely, collaborative working relationships among other government agencies (OGAs). At the PO force commander level, the establishment of coordinating centers, such as CMOCs, is one means of harmonizing the efforts of OGAs, IGOs, and nongovernmental organizations (NGOs).

g. **Host Nation (HN) Coordination.** US agencies must coordinate with HNs via the US Embassy en route to, within, and returning from the PO area. These efforts may also need to be coordinated with multinational partners providing forces and/or logistic support that traverse other nations' territories, and should be secured for the planned duration of the PO.

h. **Nongovernmental Organizations and Intergovernmental Organizations.** In many cases, adverse humanitarian conditions arising from natural or man-made disasters or conditions such as human suffering, disease, violations of human rights, civil wars, or privation that presents a serious threat to life or loss of property will characterize the PO environment.

(1) PO force commanders coordinate their efforts not only with the sponsoring organization, other militaries, and HN, but also with a myriad of NGOs, IGOs, and other agencies involved in relieving adverse humanitarian conditions. Structures like the CMOC or a CIMIC center are specifically designed to facilitate this process.

(2) It is in the military's best interest to allow NGOs and IGOs to assume primary responsibility for the FHA role and assume leadership in humanitarian emergencies as well as the disaster/emergency response mission and the long-term development missions. The United States Agency for International Development (USAID) is a primary donor for NGOs, and the PO force commander should seek out the USAID Mission for the information on the NGOs operating in the theater. Additionally, in a UN setting, the Office for the Coordination of Humanitarian Affairs (OCHA) will play a leading role. Recent developments such as the new UN "cluster system" for coordinating the efforts of numerous actors in key relief sectors may help ease coordination through the designation of "cluster leads" with OCHA overall responsible for the crisis response. In large contingencies, NGOs may also have coordination offices and security offices to facilitate information-sharing with the military and other actors on the ground.

(3) NGOs may help PO force commanders and staffs to better accomplish their mission because of their familiarity with the culture, language, and sensitivities of a populace. However, caution is necessary to prevent any perception by the populace or the parties to the dispute that these organizations are part of an information-gathering mechanism. Their purpose is to address humanitarian requirements, disaster/emergency responses, and long-term development. The NGOs and IGOs may consider their neutrality, impartiality, and independence as their primary source of security. Commanders will also find that the cultures of some of these organizations differ markedly from military culture, and there may be a strong desire on their part to maintain a wide distance from military activities.

For further information on coordination, refer to JP 3-08, Interagency, Intergovernmental Organization, and Nongovernmental Organization Coordination During Joint Operations.

For further information on CMOCs, refer to JP 3-57, Civil-Military Operations.

i. **Multinational Cooperation.** Several factors are essential for success when operations are conducted in cooperation with other nations.

(1) **Respect and Professionalism.** Mutual respect for multinational partners' ideas, culture, religion, and customs as well as a demeanor of military professionalism helps establish a basis for cooperation and unity of effort. Other nations' militaries often have years of PO experience and can contribute their experiences, expertise, and training skills as well as their capabilities.

(2) **Mission Assignment.** Missions assigned by the PO force commander will be appropriate to each multinational partner's capabilities and national direction. Multinational partners should be integrated into the planning process, thus assuring both the perception and the reality of unity of effort. Language requirements and linguistic support will be an important consideration. Special operations forces (SOF) capabilities, such as liaison elements, may assist commanders in the employment of MNFs.

(3) **Management of Resources.** Multinational partners may seek assistance with logistics support or may be able to provide additional logistic support to the PO. Agreements need to be established for exchangeable or transferable commodities before operations begin and are further developed and refined throughout the operation. Legal support will be important in formulating and interpreting these agreements.

(4) **Harmony.** Personal relationships and an effective rapport established among members of a MNF at all command levels can contribute significantly to the success of the operation.

For further information on multinational coordination, refer to JP 3-16, Multinational Operations.

j. **Strategic Communication.** Strategic communication is an important element of strategic direction during all military operations. In PO, this is further complicated by the importance of credibility and legitimacy, and the multiplicity of parties and other actors involved. Public diplomacy, public affairs (PA), and IO messages must be coordinated early during the planning process. The continual sharing of information must exist during execution. Although messages may be different, they must not contradict one another or the credibility of the PO force will be lost.

For further information on strategic communication, refer to JP 3-0, Joint Operations.

(1) **Liaison.** LNOs are critical to the successful conduct of all PO, but particularly in multinational operations. In some situations, LNOs may be the only means for the commander to communicate with some members of the PO force. LNOs help coordinate a myriad of details within a joint task force (JTF), the PO headquarters, and among the multinational contingents, the sponsoring organization, US Embassy, USG agencies, international agencies, NGOs, IGOs, and other organizations.

(2) **Public Affairs.** In PO, news media coverage generally plays a major role in quickly framing public debate and shaping public opinion. Consequently, the media serves as a forum for the analysis and critique of PO. US and international public opinion affect political, strategic, and operational decisions, and ultimately the operation's success or failure. The key issue is that the legitimacy and support for a PO can be lost if PA does not receive the proper level of attention.

For additional information about PA, refer to JP 3-61, Public Affairs.

(3) **Information Operations.** Two fundamentals of PO, transparency and impartiality, must be the cornerstone of IO in a PO environment. IO must synchronize the effects of electronic warfare, operations security, computer network operations, military deception, and psychological operations (PSYOP) in coordination with civil affairs (CA) and PA to ensure consistent themes and messages are communicated to avoid credibility loss and build public confidence in their government.

For further information on IO, refer to JP 3-13, Information Operations.

k. **Force Protection (FP) and Rules of Engagement Limitations.** FP and ROE considerations are central to all aspects of PO planning and execution, particularly when the mission is a PEO or a PKO that involves interposition between former belligerent forces. The perception of a force's impartiality may also serve as a measure of FP.

For additional ROE guidance, refer to Chairman of the Joint Chiefs of Instruction (CJCSI) 3121.01B, Standing Rules of Engagement/Standing Rules for the Use of Force for US Forces.

l. **Measures of Success.** Ultimately, settlement, not victory, is the key measure of success in PO. Settlement is achieved through a combination of actions using the instruments of national and international power. A settlement reached by conciliation among the disputing parties is generally preferable to a conflict terminated by force. It is imperative that PO establish or sustain the conditions in which political and diplomatic activities may proceed. It is also important to recognize when the end state is not achievable. This may stem from such factors as a breakdown in political resolve by the parties to the dispute or a lack of support from the international community.

m. **Measure of Effectiveness (MOE).** At the military operational and tactical levels, MOE may assist commanders and political decision makers in gauging progress in the accomplishment of the mission. MOE focus on whether military efforts are having the desired result in achieving the mandate or mission specifically assigned to the force. These measures can provide commanders and higher authorities with a means to evaluate the contribution of military efforts to the more encompassing and overarching end state and are situational dependent, often requiring readjustment as changes occur and higher level political-military guidance develops. MOE are normally discrete, quantifiable, and helpful in understanding and measuring progress. MOE must not be widely published or distributed outside the PO force.

n. **Civil Disturbances.** PO inherently includes the likelihood of encountering civil disturbances. A well-handled situation can lead to an enhanced view of both the professionalism and strength of the PO force, instill confidence in democratic and law enforcement institutions involved, and result in fewer disturbances in future operations. Controlling civil disturbances includes the following actions:

(1) Isolate in time and space the trouble spot from outside influence or interaction. Use a system of multilayered checkpoints to enable the PO force to cull identifiable troublemakers from the civilians without attracting unnecessary attention and to limit and control access. Consider using helicopters and other monitoring technologies to screen the flanks.

(2) Dominate the situation through force presence. An overwhelming show of force at checkpoints, coupled with helicopter overflights, may dissuade entry into the area by potentially destabilizing elements. Unmanned aerial vehicle platforms and helicopters may provide real-time situation reports, and assist with gaining information and awareness.

(3) Maintain situational awareness.

(4) Multidimensional, multi-echeloned actions. One element may provide local security while another focuses efforts on the larger strategic or political spectrum. Use all available resources to influence the outcome, including convincing local media to avoid inflammatory broadcasts or to make broadcasts designed to quell and disperse the crowds. Multidimensional responses include the use of civil and military nonlethal capabilities.

o. **Transition Planning.** The PO force commander should eventually transfer authority and responsibilities to another military force, a government agency, a NGO, or the HN government. The PO force must carefully plan, coordinate, and manage the transition to the relieving force, agency, organization, IGO, or civilian police (CIVPOL). Commanders should plan for transition and termination before deployment or as soon as possible during the initial phase. Transitions should consider appropriate adjustment in mandate, ROE, and legal authorities and be coordinated in accordance with an IO plan. Examples of types of transitions include the following:

(1) **Transition from US unilateral to a Coalition or UN led coalition.** Some PO may begin as a unilateral mission due to necessity of the situation and could eventually transition to a coalition or UN-led PO. Operation UPHOLD DEMOCRACY is an example of such a transitional PO.

(2) **From PEO to PKO.** If consent develops and all sides demonstrate their commitment to the peace process through acts and deeds, then a PO force organized and deployed under a PEO mandate can gradually introduce those techniques appropriate to PKO.

(3) **From military to civilian control.** Transitions may involve the transfer of certain responsibilities to civilian control.

Transitions are further discussed in Chapter IV, "Peace Building."

p. **Risk of Mission Creep.** Mission creep may develop from invalid assumptions, misinterpreted intent, unrealistic development or conflicting guidance from higher authority. Mission creep can be avoided by paying attention to specified and implied tasks and to the end state. Proposed mission changes may raise questions about the commander's legal authority to act, reimbursement, and the impact on readiness due to the increased tempo of operations.

6. Command and Control for Peace Operations

a. The United States may participate in PO under various command authority arrangements. These arrangements might include:

(1) Unilateral US joint operations.

(2) Multinational operations with the US as the lead nation.

(3) Multinational operations with the US as a contingent nation.

b. In any of these arrangements, US forces will report to the US chain of command. However, in multinational PO, the US force may also report to the sponsoring IGO such as the UN, NATO, OAU, OAS, or EU. By law, the President retains command authority over US forces. However, as Commander in Chief, the President has the authority to place US forces under the operational control (OPCON) of a foreign commander when doing so serves American security interests. The greater the anticipated US military role, the less likely it will be that the US will agree to have a non-US commander exercise OPCON over US forces. Any large scale participation of US forces in a PEO that is likely to involve combat will ordinarily be conducted under US command authority.

7. Key Documents in Peace Operations

The political objectives of a particular operation guide the development of key documents that provide legal authority and define the parameters for a PO. Key documents in PO are discussed below.

a. **Mandate.** The PO force generally conducts operations based on a mandate that describes the scope of operations. The UNSC establishes mandates for UN-sponsored PO through a UN Security Council resolution (UNSCR). PO sponsored by organizations other than the UN may also be based on mandates. These mandates will usually result from treaties, accords, resolutions, or agreements of IGOs.

b. **Status-of-Forces Agreement (SOFA) or Status of Mission Agreement (SOMA) (for UN Operations).** These agreements, negotiated between the HN and the sponsoring organization on behalf of the participating countries, establish the detailed legal status of PO forces and involve close coordination among the DOS, CCDRs, the Department of Defense (DOD), and the Chairman of the Joint Chiefs of Staff (CJCS). Authority to negotiate a SOFA is held at the national level. Some specified portions of that authority have been delegated to the Joint Staff and CCDRs. Neither the PO force commander nor the staff has such authority without specific approval or delegation from higher authority. Before entering into any negotiations or agreement with another nation, consult the staff judge advocate. US forces remain subject to the Uniform Code of Military Justice, which will be administered by the appropriate US commander.

c. **Term of Reference (TOR).** The TOR is developed to govern implementation of the PO based on the mandate and the situation and may be subject to approval by the parties to the dispute in PKO. The TOR describes the mission, command relationships, organization, logistics, accounting procedures, coordination and liaison, and responsibilities of the military units and personnel assigned or detailed to the PO force. When the United States is a participant in a PO, the TOR is coordinated with the CJCS, DOD, and DOS before final approval by the Secretary of Defense.

d. **Memorandum of Understanding (MOU).** In the context of a PO, a MOU is an agreement between the sponsoring organization and contributing countries concerned primarily with logistic and administrative matters such as financial management of the PO.

e. **Rules of Engagement.** In PO, well-conceived, clearly stated, and thoroughly disseminated ROE can make the difference between mission success and failure. ROE define when and how force may be used. All commanders will assess threat capabilities and make recommendations for specific ROE through the chain of command.

(1) US commanders will be aware that PO forces from other nations may interpret ROE differently than US forces or may wish to use different ROE. During NATO operations, the applicable NATO ROE will authorize the participating nations to publish supplemental ROE guidance based upon national requirements. Commanders and their staffs must understand the limitations of their MNF, and war game solutions during planning to prevent confusion during a crisis.

(2) For PKO, ROE are normally highly restrictive and written to limit the use of force to self-defense of the force and protection of the mission.

(3) In PEO, the ROE are less restrictive on the use of force than in PKO, but are tailored to the situation. Restraint will still be a primary consideration since the transition to peace may be easier when the PO force has only used proportional and appropriate force.

For additional information refer to CJCSI 3121.01B, Standing Rules of Engagement/Standing Rules for the Use of Force for US Forces.

Examples of key documents for PO are available at https://jdeis.js.mil/other/Joint_Doctrine Homepage/Other_Publications.

Intentionally Blank

CHAPTER II
PEACEKEEPING OPERATIONS

"Peacekeeping is not a soldier's job, but only a soldier can do it."

Dag Hammarskjold
Secretary General United Nations 1953-1961

1. General

PKO consist of military support to diplomatic, informational, and economic efforts to establish or maintain peace in areas of potential or actual conflict. The United States has participated in and supported many UN-sponsored PKO.

2. Description of Peacekeeping Operations

PKO take place following diplomatic negotiation and agreement among the parties to a dispute, the sponsoring organization, and potential force-contributing nations. Before PKO begin, a credible truce or cease fire is in effect, and the parties to the dispute must consent to the operation. PKO are conducted in an open and highly conspicuous manner (transparency). A main function of the PO force is to establish a presence that inhibits hostile actions by the disputing parties and bolsters confidence in the peace process. PKO support continuing PB diplomatic and economic efforts to achieve long-term political settlements and normalized peaceful relations. Agreements often specify which nations' forces are acceptable, as well as the size and type of forces each will contribute. The United States may participate in PKO as a lead nation, as a contingent force, unilaterally, or by providing military observers (MILOBs).

3. Fundamentals of Peacekeeping Operations

a. **Consent.** PKO require an invitation, or at a minimum, consent of all the major parties to the conflict. The PO force remains effective only with this consent that includes recognition of the host government's authority.

b. **Restraint, Minimum Force, and the Nonthreatening Nature of PKO.** In PKO, minimum force imposed by the PO force along with its inherent right to self-defense, govern the nonthreatening nature of the actions taken. A major challenge during PKO is effectively dealing with situations of extreme tension and violence without becoming a participant. When the principle of restraint is lost, PKO cannot be sustained. When the operational environment does not permit restraint, a mission change or a mandate change should be requested.

c. **Impartiality, Perception, and Legitimacy.** A PO force conducting PKO does not act in support of a government or any party to a dispute; **it is entirely impartial.** If the PO force is suspected or perceived as favoring one of the parties concerned, the trust of the other party will be compromised or lost. Once lost, the PO force will find it difficult to implement the mandate. Demonstrated impartiality is essential to establish and maintain the **legitimacy** of the PKO.

4. Peacekeeping Personnel and Peace Operations Forces

US military personnel may perform a wide variety of PKO functions. They may be detailed to serve on a multinational staff or in an observer group as MILOBs. The United States may also participate in PKO by providing forces.

a. **MILOBs are unarmed** and observe, record, and report on the implementation and violations of a formal agreement. They serve as members of an observer group and carry out such tasks as vehicle patrols in sensitive areas, local negotiations between rival forces, and special investigations. Their presence is intended to be sufficient to deter violations. By providing accurate, up-to-date, and impartial reports, MILOBs help reduce the number of claims and counterclaims by the disputing parties. MILOBs rely strongly on their impartial status and a permissive PKO environment to enable execution of assigned duties. In PKO where a military force is also present, the MILOBs work in conjunction with the force but under a separate chain of command. The Secretary of the Army (SECARMY) is the DOD executive agent for DOD support to UN missions. As such, SECARMY is responsible for the administration of personnel support to the US Military Observer Group — Washington (USMOG-W). DOD Directives (DODDs) charge the SECARMY with the following in relation to MILOBs (see DODD 2065.1E, *Assignment of Personnel to United Nations Missions*, for additional detail).

(1) Ensure that mission requirements and the administrative and logistics needs of all DOD personnel serving in UN missions are met through the USMOG-W.

(2) The USMOG-W, acting on behalf of SECARMY assumes responsibility for implementation. When directed by the Under Secretary of Defense for Policy, SECARMY coordinates with the Secretaries of other Military Departments and heads of DOD agencies to provide personnel to support PO. US MILOBs perform observer duties under the control of the observer group chief of staff or PO force commander designated by the sponsoring organization. When detailed as MILOBs, US personnel do not normally report to the GCC.

b. The force size and mix will vary depending on the mission, mandate, and threat in the operational area. Forces for PKO may include units or personnel with specialized abilities such as language skills, engineering, decontamination, explosive ordnance disposal (EOD), PSYOP, and CA. Forces employed for PKO are generally lightly armed and should be mobile, capable of self-defense, and self-sufficient until logistic resupply channels can be established.

(1) **Ground forces** may supervise or assist in the separation of opposing sides in order to establish a buffer zone (BZ) or demilitarized zone (DMZ). The PO force controls and surveys the line of demarcation, which facilitates the disengagement and withdrawal of disputing party forces, discourages infiltration confrontations, and assists in resolving local disputes. Ground operations will involve observation and monitoring of military and paramilitary units within a specified area. Military police/security force (MP/SF) units, in particular, have experience in exercising authority in tense circumstances without escalating tension. Their image as a police force, rather than a combat force, may help defuse tensions. Ground force support capabilities include those in Figure II-1.

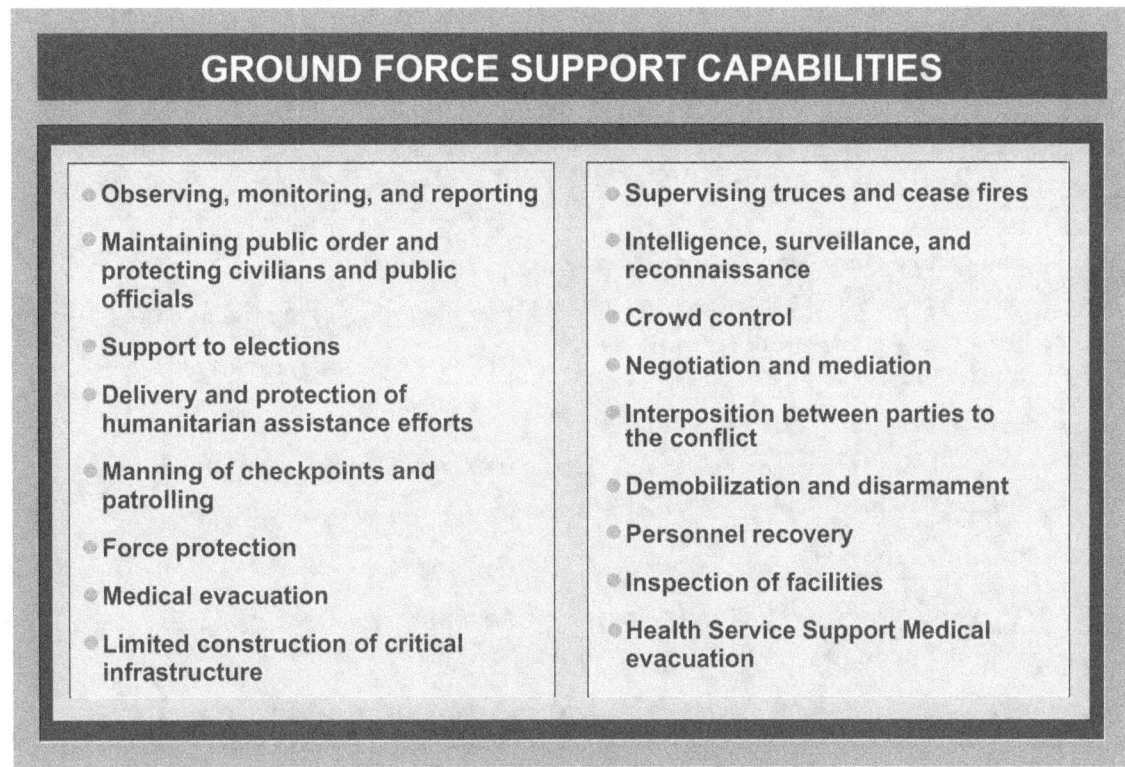

Figure II-1. Ground Force Support Capabilities

(2) **Air forces** conduct air operations which provide the speed, range, and flexibility to rapidly cover large areas. In PKO, air forces can meet a wide range of operational requirements. These include the air forces support capabilities listed in Figure II-2.

(3) **Maritime forces** provide support capabilities listed in Figure II-3. They also conduct or augment ground and air forces support capabilities (e.g., delivery of humanitarian aid; combat air patrol; intelligence, surveillance, and reconnaissance; medical evacuation; personnel recovery). Additionally, maritime forces can provide harbor movement control and port security to safeguard vessels, harbors, waterfront facilities, and cargo. Maritime forces may also conduct operations on inland waterways. The US Coast Guard (USCG) may provide additional support capabilities.

(4) **SOF personnel can play a significant role in PKO** because of their unique capabilities, training, and experience. SOF often have detailed regional knowledge of cultures and languages, as well as experience working with indigenous forces. SOF can form small, versatile, self-contained units that can rapidly deploy, and provide a full spectrum of air, ground, and maritime support with links to space-based assets. SOF capabilities are particularly important in PO for their understanding of the complexity of operating in cross-cultural environments. Due to limited numbers of SOF personnel and high demands, commanders should ensure that tasks are appropriate for SOF employment.

For further guidance on special operations capabilities, refer to JP 3-05, Doctrine for Joint Special Operations.

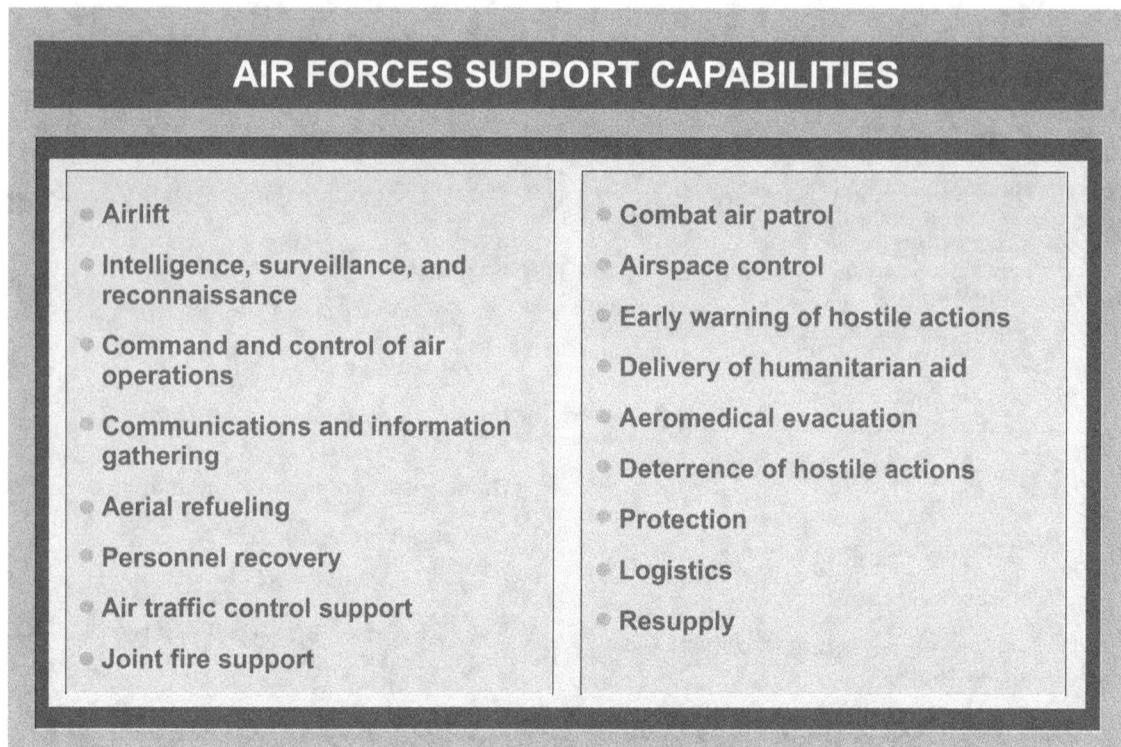

Figure II-2. Air Forces Support Capabilities

(5) **PSYOP units can assist in facilitating cooperation** between the disputing parties, their supporters, and the PO force. PSYOP can help create favorable attitudes and behavior on the part of disputing parties and uncommitted segments of the population. For example, PSYOP personnel may provide the capability to develop, produce, and disseminate a wide variety of products to inform all parties, including neutrals, about the role of the PO force, the requirements of the mandate, locations of critical services, and information that can assist in bridging cross-cultural gaps between PO forces and indigenous populations.

For additional information on PSYOP, refer to JP 3-53, Doctrine for Joint Psychological Operations.

(6) **In PKO, CA teams** provide PO force commanders with the following: area assessments; cultural awareness training; liaison and coordination among US, multinational, and indigenous forces; advice and assistance in handling dislocated civilians (DCs); coordination of host-nation support (HNS); and the establishment of CMOCs. Civil affairs operations (CAO) requires careful consideration to prevent the risk of appearing partial to one or more disputing parties. Such activities may include advice or assistance to help the HN provide for governance, rule of law, and economic stability; health and welfare; infrastructure, education, and public information.

For additional information on CMO and CAO, refer to JP 3-57, Civil-Military Operations.

MARITIME FORCES SUPPORT CAPABILITIES

- Port security and port safety services

- Coastal sea control and harbor defense services

- Maritime law enforcement

- Environmental defense and pollution prevention, migration, monitoring, and response

- Vessel traffic control and aids to navigation

- Reflagging of merchant vessels

- Training (law enforcement, search and rescue, environmental protection, port safety and security, waterway management, and maritime safety)

- Port visits

- Maritime search and rescue

- Coastal patrol and surveillance

- Staging, sustainment, and a reinforcement platform for joint forces

- Escort for shipping

- Neutral location for negotiations

- Protection of offshore and onshore assets

- Maritime interception operations

- Monitor and enforce exclusive economic zones

- Mining operations and clearing waterborne minefields

- Secure holding facility

- Secure rest and recuperation facility

Figure II-3. Maritime Forces Support Capabilities

5. **Peacekeeping Tasks**

PKO tasks will usually involve observing and monitoring, or supervising and assisting parties to a dispute.

a. **Observation and Monitoring.** Observation and monitoring tasks are performed primarily by unarmed MILOBs, but may also be performed by PO forces. In either case, they help ensure the agreements are followed by the parties to the dispute. UN observer groups may also use civilian personnel or police as observers. The success of these missions is dependent on the willingness of the disputing parties to comply with the terms of the accord or agreement. This willingness may exist because MILOBs have established a visible presence and are able to detect violations of agreements. Typical observation activities include:

(1) **Observing, monitoring, verifying, and reporting any alleged violation of the governing agreements.** Agreements may include treaties, truces, cease fires, arms control agreements, or any other binding agreements between the disputing parties.

(2) **Investigating alleged cease fire violations, boundary incidents, and complaints.** This may include incidents, unauthorized troop movements, and construction or reinforcing of

defensive positions. An investigation provides evidence regarding violations of the agreements and may involve negotiation or mediation, to include direct dialogue between the disputing parties.

(3) **Negotiating and mediating.** MILOBs may undertake negotiations on behalf of the disputing parties to mediate low-level disputes. Reconciliation of differences at the lowest possible level often contributes to the overall success of the PKO.

(4) **Conducting regular liaison visits** within the operational area. Disputes thrive on rumors, uncertainty, and prejudice. Therefore, liaison visits maintain personal contact and allow for a timely and routine exchange of information with disputing parties, the HN, local civilian officials, NGOs, IGOs, PO force headquarters, and other national contingents.

(5) **Maintaining up-to-date information on the disposition of disputing forces** within the operational area. This requires periodically visiting forward positions to observe and report on the disposition of forces of the disputing parties.

(6) **Verifying** the storage or destruction of certain categories of military equipment specified in the relevant agreements.

b. **Supervision and Assistance.** Supervision and assistance missions are normally performed by lightly armed PO forces. The PO forces undertaking these tasks require, in most cases, large service support organizations, equipment, and finances. In addition to the tasks performed by MILOBs in observation missions, PO forces may perform the tasks described below:

(1) **Supervising cease fires.** Once a cease fire is arranged, PO forces may observe and report on the disputing parties' compliance with a cease fire. The force may have to deploy on the territory of more than one nation to perform its mission. The tempo and outcome of diplomatic activities taken to establish a credible cease fire are often unpredictable, and negotiations to constitute and insert a PO force may occur simultaneously. Therefore, rapid deployment of the PO force is generally required.

(2) **Supervising disengagements and withdrawals.** If required, establishment of a BZ between disputed parties is a high priority to help ensure an uneventful disengagement and withdrawal. PO force personnel may mediate disagreements in the positioning of the disputing parties' forces, verify troop and equipment dispositions and, if authorized, provide assistance to the civilian population in the BZ.

(3) **Supervising detainee exchanges.** At any stage in the resolution of a dispute, PO forces may supervise and assist in detainee exchanges between the parties.

(4) **Supervising demobilization and demilitarization.** The parties to the dispute may agree to demobilization or demilitarization of their forces. Therefore, PO forces may supervise and assist in these activities and provide progress reports to the sponsoring organization.

(5) **Assisting civil authorities.** PO forces may assist civil authorities in such functions as supervision of elections, transfer of authority, partitioning of territory, evacuation, convoy escort, or the temporary administration of civil functions. CA units, in coordination with the CMOC, can provide advice and assistance in the execution of these functions.

(6) **Assisting in the maintenance of public order.** PO forces may assist in the reestablishment or maintenance of public order. The responsibility for public order rests primarily with the CIVPOL. However, military assistance may be required if there has been a breakdown in the CIVPOL structure or situations are beyond their capacity to control.

(7) **Supporting FHA operations.** Although FHA is not a PO, it may be necessary for PO forces to provide security for, as well as to supervise the offloading and transfer of relief supplies until FHA operations are fully established. It may also be necessary for PO forces to provide transportation and security for IGOs, NGOs, and other agencies. CA teams provide the commander a resource for the planning and conduct of FHA.

For further guidance on FHA, refer to JP 3-29, Foreign Humanitarian Assistance.

6. Command and Control for Peacekeeping Operations

Command and control (C2) relationships are established prior to the PKO in the appropriate operation plan, order, directive, or other authoritative correspondence. With continual **mission analysis** and revised plans crucial in any military operation, the C2 relationships may be adjusted to the situation.

a. **US Policy.** The President retains command authority over US forces assigned as a contingent to a MNF conducting PO. The US contingent commander remains within the US chain of command. On a case-by-case basis, the President will consider placing appropriate US forces under the OPCON of a multinational force commander (MNFC).

b. **UN Policy.** UN PKO are established by the Security Council and fall under its authority. The UN Secretary-General (UNSG) is responsible to the Security Council for the organization, conduct, and direction of the operation, and he or she alone reports to the Security Council. The UNSG is responsible for implementing UNSCRs or mandates and for monitoring all UN PKO. The UNSG will appoint a UN PO force commander and a UN Special Representative. The UN PO force commander is a military officer from a nation not involved in the dispute, whose qualifications are acceptable to the UNSC. Additionally, the UN PO force commander must also be acceptable to the HN and all the parties to the dispute.

(1) The special representative of the Secretary-General (SRSG) is normally a career diplomat who is usually the head of mission (HOM). The UN PO force commander is responsible to the UN mission's special representative for ensuring military activities support other components of the mission.

(2) The US contingent commander may be under the OPCON of the UN PO force commander, however US forces will remain within the US chain of command.

c. **Multinational PO Force Headquarters.** There is no standard staff organization for a multinational headquarters conducting a PO. However, a PO headquarters staff is normally grouped into three main categories.

(1) The MNFC's **personal staff** normally consists of a military assistant, a political adviser, a legal adviser, a PA officer, an interpreter, and LNOs from the armed forces of the parties to the dispute.

(2) The MNF **military staff** normally consists of a chief of staff, a deputy chief of staff, and functional staff elements such as operations, intelligence, plans, training, communications, administration, manpower, and logistics. The military staff may also include air traffic control, security, police operations, observer groups, health service support (HSS), and CMO. Linguists should be included to facilitate communications.

(3) The **civilian staff**, provided by the UN Secretariat in New York, at a minimum, consists of a chief administrative officer (UN). The chief administrative officer (UN) is responsible for the direction of all administrative matters having financial management implications, as well as for the overall direction of the force's administration.

d. **Command.** The MNFC may be given OPCON over US and other military units assigned to the PO force. The MNFC will ensure that the national contingent commanders perform assigned tasks consistent with the mandate and the PO force's mission.

(1) A national contingent consists of a nation's entire contribution. National contingent commanders are responsible for disciplinary action within their own contingents in accordance with their national military law. The authority for national contingent commanders to carry out their national laws in the HN's territory should be included in the SOFA and/or SOMA for the PKO. The PO force commander may discuss a major disciplinary breach with a contingent commander or, if applicable and warranted, may refer the matter to the SRSG.

(2) Each contingent commander is responsible for accomplishing assigned tasks, communicating changes in the situation, and responding to the needs and the directives of the PO force commander. Figure B-1 in Appendix B, "Command Relationships," shows a notional chain of command for PKO.

e. **Commanders' Directives.** The PO force commander's directive should clearly outline who is empowered to give orders to contingents and under what circumstances. US contingent commanders may issue their own directives based on their own mission analysis and the PO force commander's directive. A PO force commander's directive should include:

(1) The degree of command and control the force commander has over national contingents by covering such topics as:

        (a) Appointment and authority of the peace operations force commander.

        (b) Applicability of national laws and regulations to personnel in the various contingents.

        (c) Support responsibilities and procedures.

     (2) Appointment of subordinate commanders, especially those detached from the main body.

     (3) Individuals authorized to issue directives and instructions to the unit, as well as under what circumstances.

     (4) Subunit operational areas and tasks.

     (5) Methods of operation and deployment.

     (6) Reserve forces.

     (7) States of readiness.

     (8) Succession to command.

     (9) Location of forces and unit headquarters.

     (10) Peace operations force composition.

     (11) Identification; for example, the wearing of peace operations force distinctive identification (headgear, badges, and armbands), marking of vehicles and positions, and so forth.

     (12) Duration of duty and policies on liberty and rest and recreation.

     (13) Relationship with the host government and its local administration, armed forces, and police; and other organizations and agencies in the operational area.

     (14) Powers of search and seizure and rights of entry.

     (15) Media relations, including guidance on when and through whom operational information may be provided.

     (16) Force protection measures, to include information and communications security.

     (17) Regulations and restrictions to be observed off duty.

7. Peacekeeping Planning Considerations

The planning process for PKO is similar to any other military operation. However, a PKO may be initiated on relatively short notice, requiring extraordinary effort to develop a complete plan, identify, and build a headquarters staff.

For further guidance on planning joint operations, refer to JP 5-0, Joint Operation Planning, *and JP 3-33,* Joint Task Force Headquarters.

a. **The mandate, TOR, and SOFA** are important sources of information for mission analysis and planning. Additionally, commanders and staffs may gain valuable insights by reviewing the lessons learned from previous PKO or training exercises.

b. The duration of many PKO, number of participating multinational contingents, local cultural taboos, and rotation policies make standard operating procedures (SOPs) especially useful.

Examples of key documents for PO are available at https://jdeis.js.mil/other/ Joint_Doctrine_Homepage/Other_Publications.

c. When practical, the JFC should consider having the staff develop an area information handbook. The purpose would be to orient joint force members to the mission, operational area, history of the conflict and its parties, religious and cultural factors, and other important information about the environment in which they will be operating. Other sources include: PA, intelligence personnel, foreign area officers, CA, Army Special Forces, and PSYOP forces.

d. Successful planning and employment requires **detailed coordination at all levels**. Therefore, **LNOs should be identified** to assist the commander and staff as they coordinate plans and actions among the peacekeeping contingents, UN or sponsoring organizations, IGOs, NGOs, other agencies, and local authorities. The latter may include military leaders, local officials, customs, transportation authorities, and police. A CMOC provides a venue for coordination between the military and these personnel.

e. **Logistics.** There are some differences in how logistic support is provided in PKO. Consequently, logisticians' involvement in the planning process from the very beginning will help to ensure mission success. The ad hoc and multinational nature of PKO demands careful and detailed logistic planning. This is particularly true in UN-sponsored PKO.

(1) **In UN PKO**, the deployed elements of the UN Field Administration and Logistics Division make arrangements for goods and services common to all the contingents, such as for water, some food items, fuel, and billeting. However, the UN requires time to contract for this support. Consequently, when PO forces initially deploy they should, to the extent possible, be self-sufficient for a minimum of 60-90 days. National contingents are responsible for all logistic support that is unique to their requirements. Normally, US forces will be supported through a combination of scheduled US resupply, contingency contracting, HNS, and UN logistic support.

Other logistic considerations for multinational operations include the possibility of role specialization and a lead nation provider for certain classes of supply or services.

(2) In **non-UN-sponsored operations**, a single nation may be responsible for planning and coordinating logistic support for the PO force. For example, in the multinational force and observers in the Sinai, the United States is responsible for logistic support to all national contingents, to include supply, transportation, maintenance, communications, small arms maintenance, movement control, financial management, postal, HSS, EOD, and mortuary affairs. However, many of these requirements may be satisfied through commercial contracts and require reimbursements from the participating or requesting nations or agencies.

(3) In PKO, **contracting for support will generally be necessary**. Contracting may include theater support contracting through a Service or joint contingency contracting support organization or from a Service management external support contract such as the Army's logistics civil augmentation program (LOGCAP), the Navy's global contingency construction contract program, and the Air Force contract augmentation program (AFCAP). Effective advance parties include contracting personnel to assure the necessary level of support for the US contingent force. Planners should also be aware that in some regions, reliability and timeliness of contractor performance may not be the same as in developed areas. When the United States participates in a UN PKO, direct coordination between US military planning staffs and UN planners should be authorized to ensure effective and responsive support to US forces.

For further guidance on contracting, refer to JP 4-10, Contracting and Contractor Management in Joint Operations.

(4) **For UN PKO, many of the costs incurred by the United States are reimbursable by the UN.** The UN issues detailed guidance explaining the logistic support provided by the UN and the procedures for participating nations to follow to receive reimbursement for other support. US units that participate in UN PKO must provide a detailed accounting for all costs incurred in the operations to justify UN reimbursement. UN and US, or US and coalition standards for various types of logistic support may be different, and special costs and complications may ensue. Advanced determination of these differences is important. In any case, specific agreements should spell out exactly who is to provide specified support to whom, for what period, and in what quantities. CA and CMO staff should be involved in any logistic efforts involving HN or civilian personnel.

(5) **PKO are often conducted in logistically austere theaters where there may be limited or inadequate air and seaport facilities.** If the HN has insufficient capability or capacity to support offloading at their ports, US support personnel must deploy before the scheduled arrival of the US contingent force. In some cases, existing facilities may require expansion or new facilities constructed to handle incoming forces. It also may require joint logistics over-the-shore operations. Repositioning of additional materials handling equipment may also be necessary.

(6) **Logistic planners will also determine** if existing bilateral HNS agreements containing logistic support provisions applicable to the sustainment of US contingent forces are

adequate. If not in existence, then logisticians should be actively involved in their formulation, a process that may take 12-24 months. Activation of HNS agreements are not necessarily automatic during PKO. Approval by the concerned governments may be necessary.

For detailed information on multinational logistic planning, refer to JP 4-08, Joint Doctrine for Logistic Support to Multinational Operations.

f. **Intelligence and Information Gathering.** The overt collection of information that is readily available or observable is a normal practice used by all and when reported can constitute significant intelligence information. However, sensitivities exist about use of the term "intelligence" in PKO. Intelligence support can also assess the needs of the population, infrastructure, and the effects of politics, history, and culture. Commanders and their staffs must seek to share information and intelligence with other contingents of the multinational peacekeeping force, and selected IGOs and NGOs while protecting sources and methods.

For further guidance on intelligence support, refer to JP 2-01, Joint and National Intelligence Support to Military Operations.

g. **Communication Systems.** Attention during the planning phase to information assurance and computer network/Global Information Grid defense will facilitate cross domain information transfer and decrease the potential for DOD system compromises. Even in an unclassified environment as PO, care must be exercised to protect systems. Additionally, bandwidth requirements and capabilities should be addressed. Early and detailed discussions will prevent unmet expectations for communications support.

For additional information see JP 6-0, Joint Communication Systems.

h. **Force Protection.** FP is a high priority for a deployed PO force. Strict impartiality, as previously mentioned, may reduce the threat to the PO force. ROE are also an essential element of FP and will provide for appropriate action to protect the force. The US contingent commander is responsible for setting and enforcing standards of physical security for US forces in coordination with the PO force commander and the supported CCDR. Some FP considerations include the following:

(1) Coordination with HN civil police, supporting MP, CA teams, and PSYOP units.

(2) Terrorism poses serious problems for the PKO. Effective antiterrorism measures should be planned and executed to reduce this threat. Adequate precautions will protect personnel, positions, headquarters, transportation assets, infrastructure, facilities, and billets.

For further guidance on antiterrorism, refer to JP 3-07.2, Antiterrorism.

(3) The PO force may become a target for criminal activity and/or a desperate populace.

(4) Vulnerability to attacks with mines; improvised explosive devices; rocket propelled grenades; or mortars.

(5) PO forces have limited authority to check the backgrounds of local employees.

(6) PO forces may have limited communications-security capabilities.

(7) Modifying the FP plan at irregular intervals may offer the PO force commander levels of protection not afforded by retaining the original plan and executing it in the same manner repeatedly.

i. **PKO Reserve Forces.** Although the UN utilizes multinational reserves, the US contingent commander may also designate a US reserve. The US contingent reserve should be sufficiently armed, trained, equipped, funded, advantageously located, and mobile. When deployed under normal circumstances, the reserve will deploy in a high profile, nontactical manner with the UN or PO force flag clearly displayed. The US contingent commander will commit his reserve as necessary in order to accomplish the mission. In the event the UN contingent reserve cannot resolve the incident, the PO force commander may request the US reserve force.

j. **Contingency Planning.** These plans may include states of readiness, evacuation, disaster plans, and procedures for handling displaced civilians and requests for asylum.

(1) **The PO force headquarters will establish states of readiness.** The states of readiness may vary from force to force, but UN PO forces normally have three states of readiness: normal vigilance, increased vigilance, and full alert. Each increase in the state of readiness will be complemented by restrictions on rest and recuperation (R&R), training, and certain operations. Changes in the states of readiness are normally implemented only by the PO force commander. In an emergency, the US contingent commander may order a higher state of readiness, but must immediately inform the PO force headquarters.

(2) **A PO force may need to be evacuated if armed conflict breaks out or the disputing parties withdraw consent.** Evacuation of the entire PO force may be ordered by the appropriate authority; i.e., the UNSC or the sponsoring organization. If ordered to evacuate, the PO force commander is responsible for the safe and speedy evacuation of the PO force, visitors, observer groups in the area, and personnel affiliated with the sponsoring organization. The US contingent commander will plan for the possibility that the US contingent may need to be evacuated unilaterally. In this instance, the US contingent commander will coordinate with the PO force headquarters to determine if the contingent's positions and tasks are to be handed over to another contingent or abandoned. The US contingent commander will coordinate evacuation plans with the supported GCC who has responsibility to evacuate the US contingent. Evacuation plans include specific instructions for destroying critical items, equipment, and other assets that cannot be removed. Every attempt must be made to evacuate HSS supplies and equipment. Those items which cannot be evacuated will be abandoned; however, such abandonment is a command decision. HSS supplies and equipment are afforded protection under the provisions of the Geneva Conventions and may not be intentionally destroyed.

(3) **Disasters.** Contingency plans address procedures to respond to potential **natural or man-made disasters**. CA and PSYOP forces can provide the interface with civilian authorities and indigenous populations and institutions (IPI). Personnel accountability procedures must be addressed.

(4) **DCs can pose significant challenges.** The TOR and SOP should identify procedures for handling refugees, evacuees, expellees, and other DCs. Commanders must determine the capability of care required to support these operations, especially preventive medicine, and should consider the fiscal authority to render humanitarian assistance (HA). A determination must be made on the eligibility of personnel for care by the PO force. MP, CA teams, and tactical PSYOP units are trained to assist in these activities.

Refer to JP 3-57, Joint Doctrine for Civil-Military Operations.

(5) **Granting requests for asylum can compromise the impartiality of the PO force.** Handling of such requests should be outlined in the PO force SOPs or other document available to commanders.

k. **Special Considerations.** A number of special considerations apply to PKO. The following are examples:

(1) PO force personnel will be required to conduct many independent actions involving a high degree of professionalism, self-discipline, flexibility, patience, and tact.

(2) PO force personnel will encounter differences in cultural norms, work ethics, and standards of professionalism among other national contingents; these differences require understanding and respect.

(3) The PO force will have an impact on the local economy. Although the presence of the PO force may stimulate growth in the local economy, commanders must also be aware of the potential negative impacts on the economy after the PO force departs. Policies may be developed to reduce these impacts, such as regulating the amount of dollars US personnel are allowed to convert to local currency and paying local civilians hired to support the US contingent force the prevailing wages for the area. The policy on leave, pass, liberty, and R&R should also consider these economic impacts.

(4) PO forces may wish to avoid the development of elaborate base camps and support facilities that may lead to a perception of a permanent presence by the local population.

(5) Coordination with other USG agencies, IGOs, NGOs, and UN agencies will be an important part of the PKO.

(6) HSS assistance to the local population or other contingents may become part of the mission, requiring advanced planning for legality and procedures.

(7) Nonlethal weapons give commanders a wider array of options in developing and implementing measured responses to a given situation. Use of nonlethal weapons requires special training to ensure they are properly used and effectively integrated with other capabilities.

8. Employment

a. PKO include separation of the parties to the dispute, patrolling, and observing and reporting on compliance with or violations of agreements. To successfully perform their mission, forces conducting PKO must have freedom of movement, open access to all areas in their operational area, and the ability to freely patrol, observe, monitor, verify, and report their findings.

b. A PO force may be employed in one of two ways: each national contingent is allocated to a specific operational area, or the national contingents rotates among the operational areas. Normally the first way is preferred. PKO heavily depends on accurate human intelligence (HUMINT). These sources are developed over time and involve the entire PKO organization.

(1) Assignment to a Specific Operational Area

(a) The key advantage is that each national contingent develops in-depth knowledge of the terrain and community in its specific operational area. This results in continuity in collecting and processing information. Additionally, useful relationships are developed with the local authorities of the host government, police, and leadership of the parties to the dispute. PO forces become attuned to the normal activities in the area and consequently can quickly detect changes to normal routines. Forces become well-acquainted with the local forces and are able to recognize and prohibit military personnel of the opposing forces from passing through checkpoints.

(b) The disadvantage is that national contingents may become overly familiar with the people in the area due to habitual contact, and as a result may liberally interpret agreements and enforcement policies in their operational area. This may lead to a perception of partiality and compromise mission accomplishment. If actual or perceived inequities exist, the parties to the dispute may request an exchange of contingent forces. An additional risk is that, over time, the force may become complacent in its tactical mission execution.

(2) Rotation Among Operational Areas

(a) The key advantage is that each contingent obtains a working knowledge of more than one area. The potential for forces to become overly familiar with parties to the dispute is also reduced.

(b) There are several disadvantages. A national contingent may not have sufficient time to acquire an in-depth knowledge of the area or community. Important background information gathered by a national contingent may not be effectively passed to succeeding national contingents due to language differences and different ways of operating. Rotation may also disrupt logistic operations and HUMINT collection efforts. With each rotation of national contingents, even slight differences in how the peacekeepers operate may cause distress for the local populace.

c. **Separation of Parties to the Dispute.** Many PKO will require the contingent forces to supervise the orderly disengagement and withdrawal of the parties to the dispute. The direct intervention of these forces may be required to defuse sensitive or potentially explosive situations. It will also give the disputing parties the confidence that their withdrawal will not be used to the advantage of another disputing party or parties.

For additional information see Field Manual (FM) 3-07.31, Marine Corps Warfighting Publication (MCWP) 3-33.8, Air Force Tactics, Techniques, and Procedures (Instruction) (AFTTP(I)) 3- 2.40, Multi-Service Tactics, Techniques, and Procedures for Conducting Peace Operations.

CHAPTER III
PEACE ENFORCEMENT OPERATIONS

"Diplomacy is utterly useless where there is no force behind it."

Theodore Roosevelt
June 2, 1897

1.   Description of Peace Enforcement Operations

a. PEO enforce the provisions of a mandate designed to maintain or restore peace and order. PEO may include the enforcement of sanctions and exclusion zones, protection of FHA, restoration of order, and forcible separation of belligerent parties. PEO may be conducted pursuant to a lawful mandate or in accordance with international law and do not require the consent of the HN or the parties to the conflict, although broad based consent is preferred. Forces conducting PEO use force or the threat of force to coerce or compel compliance with resolutions or sanctions. In PEO, force is threatened against or applied to belligerent parties to terminate fighting, restore order, and create an environment conducive to resolving the dispute. Although combat may be required, PEO are not classified as major operations and normally have more restrictive ROE. Forces conducting PEO generally have full combat capabilities, although there may be some restrictions on weapons and targeting.

b. Conduct of PEO is normally governed by UN Charter Chapter VII (by a regional organization or lead nation designated by the UN), but in rare situations may be conducted under the basis of collective self-defense by a regional organization, a lead nation-led coalition, or unilaterally by the US. PEO do not require the consent of the HN or the parties to the conflict, and to that end they may appear to disregard state sovereignty. The 2004 UNSG's "High-level Panel on Threats Challenges and Change," cognizant of this issue, established an international criteria for such intervention. A state can fail to meet its inherent sovereignty obligation to protect its own people and not threaten its neighbors and the international community. In such circumstances, the international community can legally use force in accordance with the criteria contained in UN Charter, Chapter VII. See: http://www.un.org/secureworld/report.pdf.

c. In a PEO the use of force is NOT limited to self-defense.

d. PEO contingent forces may have to fight their way into the conflict area and use force to separate the combatants physically.

e. The operational area will normally include civilians that pose special considerations such as threat identification, collateral damage, civilian casualties, and other issues associated with DCs.

f. Participation in PEO with multinational partners involves several unique factors for the PO force commander to consider. Certain multinational partners, for example, may not have a vital national interest at stake in the conflict or may even face certain dilemmas in regard to their involvement. Consequently, the partners' resolve may be reduced by factors such as casualties, protracted involvement, or financial management costs. Some MNFs may not possess sufficient military capabilities to conduct PEO. The challenge to the PO force commander is to constitute a PO force capable of coordinated and sustained offensive and defensive operations as required.

2. Fundamentals of Peace Enforcement Operations

In addition to the fundamentals already discussed in Chapter I, "Primer for Peace Operations," the following amplifications are made specifically for PEO.

a. **Consent.** In PEO, consent of the parties to the dispute is not a requirement, although some parties may extend it. At the strategic level, consent should, but may not, translate to the tactical level, where local groups could still disagree violently with their leaders

b. In PEO, **impartiality** still requires the PO force to act on behalf of the peace process and mandate, and not show preference for any faction or group over another. Because PEO will use coercive force and intervene against the will of some, many people may perceive that the PO force is not impartial. Therefore the PO force must focus IO to counter these perceptions.

c. **Restraint and Minimum Force.** A misuse of force can have a negative impact upon the legitimacy of the PO. On the other hand, the appropriate use of force to prevent disruption of the peace process can strengthen consent. The PO force uses situational understanding to include cultural, sociological, religious, and ethnic aspects to determine how best to use this force. When used, force (lethal and nonlethal) should be no more than is necessary and proportionate to resolve and defuse a crisis. The force used must be limited to the degree, intensity, and duration required to remove the threat and prevent further escalation.

3. Peace Enforcement Operations Tasks

PEO tasks may include some of those conducted in PKO as well as enforcement of sanctions and exclusion zones, protection of FHA, operations to restore order, and forcible separation of belligerent parties or parties to a dispute.

a. **Enforcement of sanctions and exclusion zones** includes a broad range of possible tasks. Commanders must understand that actions to enforce sanctions, while endorsed by the UNSC, have traditionally been considered **acts of war** and should posture their forces accordingly.

b. PEO contingent forces may be tasked to **provide protection** for FHA missions. This could include protection for IGOs, NGOs, OGAs, and other military personnel who are providing FHA. Such protection may include establishing secure base areas, protecting routes or corridors for the transport of relief supplies, and providing security for distribution sites. If belligerent parties oppose the delivery of relief supplies by IGOs, NGOs, or other agencies, PEO forces may deliver the supplies by providing airlift or other forms of logistic support. The CMOC, when established, serves as the focal point for requests for support from US forces.

c. **Operations to restore order** are conducted to halt violence and support, reinstate, or establish civil authorities. They are designed to restore stability to the point where indigenous police forces can effectively enforce the law and reinstate civil authority.

d. **Forcible Separation of Belligerent Parties.** This PEO task can pose a very high risk to the contingent force. Forcible separation may involve reducing the combat capability of one or more of the belligerent parties. The contingent force will normally retain the right of first use of force. Forces conducting forcible separation require extensive offensive combat capability, as well as combat support and combat service support (CSS). The goal is to force the belligerent parties to disengage, withdraw and, subsequently, to establish a BZ or DMZ.

e. **Conduct internment/resettlement (I/R) operations.** If PEO require forcible separation of belligerent parties, then there will be a requirement to conduct I/R operations as contingent forces capture or detain parties to the conflict. Depending on the type of conflict that results from forcible separation, I/R operations will need to be conducted for enemy prisoners of war/ civilian internees and/or DCs. Forces responsible for conducting I/R operations must ensure that appropriate CSS assets are deployed to support this PO mission. The I/R operations will become critical as forces transition from PEO to PKO.

4. **Command and Control for Peace Enforcement Operations**

In most cases, PEO mirror conventional military operations and possess many of the same C2 characteristics. The fundamentals of PO, discussed in Chapter I, "Primer for Peace Operations," are germane. Unity of effort, especially, is important when planning command arrangements, international agreements, and coordination centers and cells.

a. For both unilateral and multinational operations, US forces will normally be structured as a JTF. The composition of the forces in the JTF will depend on the mission, concept of operations (CONOPS), and the threat.

b. For multinational PEO, PO forces may operate under a lead nation, a parallel, or a combination command structure.

(1) In the **lead nation command structure**, one nation's commander directs or leads the multinational partners in the accomplishment of the PO mission. In this context, "lead nation" can also include "lead UN" or "lead alliance," terms found in other PO documents and publications. In this publication, "lead nation" will be used and may include the other terms as appropriate. Lead UN command structure is usually under the lead of a civilian SRSG. Lead alliance command structures such as NATO are governed by standardization agreements with national elements under the direction of a standing NATO headquarters element. The lead nation normally provides the PO force commander, the basic staff, the preponderance of the PO forces, and the communications to control operations. This helps achieve unity of command and unity of effort and facilitates mutual understanding of the mandate by all partners. If the US is the lead nation, the US supported GCC or a subordinate commander will normally be designated as the PO force commander.

(2) In the **parallel command structure**, a force commander is selected by the sponsoring organization. The staff is comprised of staff members from all contributing nations and is assembled on an ad hoc basis. If any nation within a coalition elects to exercise autonomous control of its force, a parallel command structure exists. Nations retain control of their deployed forces. The coalition leadership must develop a means for coordination among the participants to attain unity of effort. This can be accomplished through the use of multinational coordinating councils at the level of the national commanders, with tactical control of individual national components being assigned to other national commanders under bilateral agreements.

(3) **Combination.** Lead nation and parallel command structures can exist simultaneously within a coalition but are uncommon in PO. This combination occurs when two or more nations serve as controlling elements for a mix of MNFs. Coordinating mechanisms need to be established to synchronize operations.

For further guidance on multinational C2, refer to JP 3-16, Multinational Operations.

5. Peace Enforcement Planning Considerations

Many planning considerations for PEO are similar to those for PKO. The planning process for PEO is the same as for any other military operation and begins with a comprehensive mission analysis. US forces are normally employed in accordance with a CONOPS that includes transition from PEO to PKO and/or PB.

For information on campaign planning, refer to JP 5-0, Joint Operation Planning.

a. **Mission Analysis.** In PEO there may be increased sensitivity with regard to political factors and constraints and restraints. Termination criteria, determined by the national objectives and end state and found in a mandate in UN operations, focus on the maintenance or restoration of international peace and security. Specific intelligence requirements are critical to a comprehensive mission analysis especially in PEO. Intelligence requirements are normally greater in PEO than in PKO since the potential for hostilities is higher and the details of information required to support decision-making, including FP issues is greater. Accurate intelligence and comprehensive mission analysis will be the basis for determining the structure and composition of the force.

b. **Intelligence**

(1) In addition to standard threat indicators and order of battle, an emphasis must be placed on determining the root causes of the problem and those factors that will help commanders influence the behavior of the belligerents.

(2) The commander requires predictive intelligence that can give indications and warning of a deteriorating situation or resumption of hostilities. As part of the joint intelligence preparation of the operational environment, probable courses of action of belligerents should be

developed and analyzed. A detailed collection plan that leverages all of the capabilities of the PEO contingent is a key to successful information collection.

c. **Fire Support.** In PEO, fire support is constrained by ROE, and a prime consideration is the need to minimize collateral damage. The objective is to compel or coerce the belligerents to disengage, withdraw, and comply with the mandate. Therefore, fire support may be directed more toward threats to the belligerent parties and suppression and neutralization than towards destruction of targets.

For additional information, refer to JP 3-09, Joint Fire Support.

d. **Logistics.** Logistic planning and support in PEO include the considerations addressed for PKO in Chapter II, "Peacekeeping Operations." The conduct of PEO, especially where active combat takes place, may complicate the work of other agencies, such as IGOs and NGOs. Consequently, the demand for food, water, billeting, waste disposal, movement control, environmental and safety concerns, and HSS supplies and services may increase substantially above the PO force's own requirements if large numbers of DCs must be supported until FHA operations are fully established. CA and the CMOC can enhance this effort and should be included in the logistic planning effort. Some general considerations for the PO force commander include:

(1) Logistics may have to support both the PO force and the FHA effort. Coordination with IGOs and NGOs will facilitate this support.

(2) Plan for PB and mission termination or PEO to PKO transition. Analyze what logistic infrastructure, materiel, capabilities, and equipment will remain in-country for use by follow-on forces or organizations. Determine requirements for redeployment of forces, materiel, and equipment.

(3) Authority over logistics under multinational and UN PO is situational. Areas which must be clarified include funding, cross-servicing, and mutual support agreements.

(4) Establishing a joint logistics center can provide necessary logistical control and coordination functions.

For additional information, refer to JP 4-0, Joint Logistic Support.

(5) PO force logisticians should have joint and multinational experience.

e. **Force Protection.** Because of the nature of PEO, PO forces often face a greater threat than in other PO; therefore, in addition to taking into account FP considerations for all PO, PEO commanders in particular must ensure that all personnel are trained on the terrorist threat and appropriate antiterrorism measures prior to and upon arrival in theater and as required during mission execution. Additionally, during PEO, IGOs, NGOs, OGAs, the media, and others may request some form of protection from military forces.

For additional information on FP, refer to JP 3-0, Joint Operations.

f. **Mobility and Survivability.** To ensure a mobile, survivable force, both engineer and chemical, biological, radiological, and nuclear (CBRN) defense forces provide essential support during PO.

(1) **Engineer Forces.** Engineers play a major role in PO by developing achievable and supportable engineer end state options. These options identify the essential missions to be executed, the force package and construction materials needed, the proposed construction standard, the estimated time required to execute the option, and any special considerations such as civic actions. Planners consider all available engineer capabilities, to include HN, other Services, coalition forces, contractors, and troop units. Planners consider the specific capability and availability of the units when building the force along with facilities available for leasing and infrastructure. Interoperability must be considered to ensure that assets are complementary, if not compatible. Engineer planners also consider personnel or material assets available through contracts, local sources, and the Services civil augmentation programs (i.e., LOGCAP, GCC, Navy global contingency construction contract program, and AFCAP).

(2) **CBRN Defense Forces.** Commanders consider the requirement for CBRN defense forces in support of PO if there is evidence that belligerent forces may employ such capabilities. In addition, when properly authorized, commanders can employ riot control agents as an alternative to deadly force in certain PO. A mix of different units (decontamination units/CBRN reconnaissance elements) are often necessary to achieve the proper balance. These capabilities may include local security, spray, storage, personnel shower, and a firefighting capability. CBRN staff officers may advise on commercial CBRN threats, as well as on the collection, packaging, storage, disposal, and clean-up of hazardous materials (HAZMAT) and/or wastes.

6. Employment

Typical phases for PEO are shown in Figure III-1. These phases and their sequencing may be different for some PEO, but they provide a starting point for the employment planning process. Figure III-1 also illustrates how the phases correspond to the 6-phase planning model discussed in JP 3-0, *Joint Operations*, and JP 5-0, *Joint Operation Planning.*

a. **Preparation and Deployment.** Considerations involve movement from marshalling areas, loading and departure from ports of embarkation, and sequenced movement of forces to the objective area. Mission analysis, available forces, and factors such as available HNS will influence deployment decisions. The critical decisions for the PO force commander are selecting the proper units and time-phasing their entry to secure the lodgment.

b. **Establishment of Presence in the Operational Area.** In this phase, military forces occupy and secure a presence in the operational area and establish security for follow-on elements.

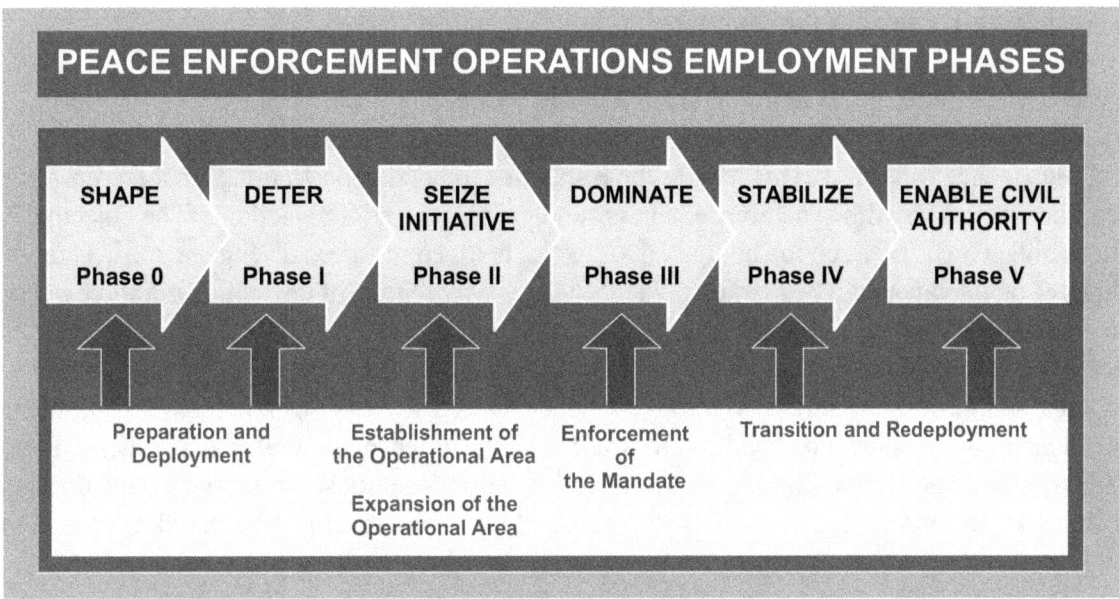

Figure III-1. Peace Enforcement Operations Employment Phases

(1) Some activities conducted during this phase include:

(a) Making contact with US and IGOs, local military and paramilitary organizations, and civil authorities.

(b) Establishing surveillance over the planned points of entry.

(c) Conducting operations to reduce the risk to the force including the use of PA and authorized IO to notify and prepare the indigenous population for the arrival of forces and contemplated actions.

(d) Providing up-to-the-minute situation reports prior to the entry of follow-on forces.

(2) The situation will dictate the nature of the initial entry forces. An unopposed entry arranged through diplomatic actions and coordination with HN or local authorities is preferred. Preservation of the HN infrastructure is a key consideration in this phase. If an opposed entry is required, forcible entry operations will be conducted prior to initiation of PKO under the provisions of JP 3-18, *Joint Forcible Entry Operations*.

c. **Expansion of the Operational Area.** In this phase, forces within the operational area continue to expand their coverage to gain information on belligerent dispositions. Staffs continue to update their information on the area and revise their assessments for operational requirements. Forces continue to arrive. When possible, theater support contracting can be used to offset the amount of logistic support which must be deployed. Air and maritime operations continue and may involve the establishment and enforcement of exclusion zones. In order to expand the operational area, air operations require protection.

d. **Enforcement of the Mandate**

(1) **Separation of Belligerent Parties.** Depending on the threat and the level of cooperation by the belligerents, the PO force conducts operations to force the belligerents to disengage and withdraw. This may involve show of force, demonstrations, or force-on-force combat operations with synchronized air, ground, maritime, and SOF actions. The objective is to establish a BZ between the belligerents. As the belligerent forces disengage and withdraw, lines of demarcation will be marked to identify the forward limits of the belligerent forces. The resulting space between these lines of demarcation constitutes a BZ. If the belligerent parties show no inclination to consent to the formation of a BZ, the PO force may establish one using combat action. In doing so, the PO force commander considers the belligerent forces' dispositions and territorial advantages or disadvantages, as well as historical or cultural considerations. Even after the situation has stabilized, belligerent parties may still demonstrate animosity toward each other and perhaps the PO force. Therefore, the PO force must remain prepared to engage in combat.

(2) **Support of Political Mediation.** The JFC will seek to thoroughly understand the political aims of the PEO and the cause and effect relationship of all actions on the resolution of the conflict. Military support may involve monitoring the compliance of belligerent parties with agreements, provisions of a mandate, or other constraints, restraints, or provisions regarding their activities.

(3) **Establishment of a Demilitarized Zone.** Negotiations may eventually transform the BZ into a DMZ, as stipulated in a formal agreement. DMZs are created to neutralize certain areas from military occupation and activity. Generally, a DMZ is in an area claimed by two or more sides in the conflict and where control by one could constitute a direct threat to the others. The boundaries of a DMZ are defined by lines of demarcation. These boundaries must be easily recognizable and, ideally, should not run counter to locally accepted political or cultural divisions. The airspace over a DMZ is denied to the aircraft of the belligerents.

(4) **Maintaining Separation of Belligerent Parties.** Security operations such as screening, combat and reconnaissance patrolling, cordon and search, and establishing checkpoints and roadblocks to control movement into and within the BZ or DMZ may be conducted to maintain the separation of belligerent parties.

(5) **Disarmament, demobilization, repatriation, reintegration, and resettlement (DDRRR) of belligerent parties** can occur concurrently with PKO and PEO. For additional information see Chapter IV, "Peace Building."

e. **Transition and Redeployment.** An effective plan for PEO will include the conditions for the eventual exit of the PO forces. This will usually be expressed as part of the military end state of the operation and will be as much of a political consideration as a military one. Once the belligerent parties agree to stop fighting by a cease fire or a truce, the stage is set for PEO to PKO transition and PB. As this agreement takes shape and the situation stabilizes, the PO force commander will begin a phased withdrawal of combat forces, which may help to defuse tensions.

Where combat may have occurred, questions about actual or perceived impartiality may preclude the PO force (particularly the combat forces) from successfully transitioning from PEO to PKO. The handover of operations and facilities should occur as a relief in place. It is important to establish liaison with and carefully synchronize the handover of PEO to PKO.

Intentionally Blank

CHAPTER IV
PEACE BUILDING

1. General

PB provides the reconstruction and societal rehabilitation that offers hope to resolve conflict. PKO and PEO include predominantly military actions that establish the conditions that enable PB (diplomatic, informational, and economic) to succeed. PB promotes reconciliation, strengthens and rebuilds civil infrastructures and institutions, builds confidence, and supports economic reconstruction to prevent a return to conflict. PB tasks are at times called "post-conflict reconstruction actions." The activities and objectives of PB are generally the same as those in stability operations. Stability operations establish the conditions that enable PB to succeed. Regardless of what term is applied to such an operation, the PB mission sectors described in this chapter are applicable. Some instability will exist concurrently with the PB. The major responsibility for PB resides ultimately with the HN and the civil sector, but the PO force has a supporting and essential role. Because the PO force and civil efforts are inextricably linked, harmony and synchronization are imperative. PB usually begins during PKO or PEO and continues after they are concluded.

2. Description of Peace Building

PB consists of actions that support political, economic, social, and security aspects of society. Although the major responsibility for PB is with the civil sector, early in PO, when critical and immediate tasks normally carried out by civilian organizations temporarily exceed their capabilities, the PO force should perform those tasks or cooperate to ensure that those tasks are accomplished. In these situations, the PO force provides immediate relief and helps to create a sustainable infrastructure. This "temporary" assumption of military responsibility for civilian tasks could range from a matter of weeks in relatively stable settings to years in an environment of ongoing security concerns. PB consists of the five mission sectors, depicted in Figure IV-1, and discussed in this chapter. It is imperative that commanders at all levels conduct a thorough mission analysis in collaboration with other appropriate national and intergovernmental agencies, for each of these sectors and understand the impact of each sector on the others.

Figure IV-1. Peace Building Mission Sectors

3. **Fundamentals of Peace Building**

a. The fundamentals of PO discussed in Chapter I, "Primer for Peace Operations," also apply to PB. One of these fundamentals, civil-military harmonization, is paramount during PB. Civil-military harmonization includes those CMO activities that promote the coordination, integration, and synchronization of civil and military efforts and actions to build the peace. These efforts and actions must occur across the various institutions and agencies at the strategic, operational, and tactical levels. The following are key considerations for the PO force commander and others involved in PB.

(1) Political leadership establishes and communicates a framework so that coordination of PO force actions with supporting multinational, OGA, IGO, and NGO participants may be harmonized.

(2) Military and civilian agencies develop complementary plans.

(3) Military and civilian agencies establish coordination mechanisms to support harmonization. A CMOC is one example; a NATO CIMIC center is another.

(4) The PO force focuses on supporting civilian agencies, organizations, and HN to assume full authority for implementing the civil portion of the peace process, while being prepared to conduct such tasks themselves in the absence of civilian agencies.

(5) Many partners from the international community, such as IGOs and NGOs, though not official implementers of national policy, may contribute to achieving the PO objectives. The

role of indigenous leaders and organizations must be considered. Appropriately harmonizing local institutions with international and military efforts is a challenging and essential task.

b. **The ultimate measures of success in PB are social, economic, and political**, not military. Therefore, the PO force commander continually seeks a clear understanding of the political objectives and strives to support their attainment.

4. Peace Building Mission Sectors

a. **Security Mission.** This sector consists of actions taken to ensure a safe and secure environment, develop legitimate and stable security institutions, and consolidate indigenous capacity. This should be complimentary and concurrent with other agencies actions that would include providing public order and safety; protecting individuals, infrastructure, and institutions; coordinating compliance through HN mechanisms such as civil military commissions; and cooperating with supportive public information programs. The goal of the PO force is to create the conditions for other political, economic, and humanitarian PB activities to achieve the political objectives stated in the mandate and to transition from military to local civil control. The PO force security tasks during PB may include:

(1) Separate and neutralize belligerent forces (normally a PEO action).

(2) Establish and maintain freedom of movement.

(3) Establish control measures for urban and rural areas, crowds, weapons, and incidents.

(4) Establish border control to prevent external support to a conflict.

(5) Protect key infrastructure, institutions, and individuals.

(6) Observe, verify, and monitor security situation.

(7) Investigate security violations.

(8) Respond to crisis.

(9) Reconstitute national armed forces and other SFs as required.

(10) DDRRR is the process of transitioning a conflict or wartime military establishment and defense-based civilian economy to a peacetime configuration, while maintaining national security and economic vitality. Sustainable peace usually requires disarmament and weapons management programs, demobilization of opposing forces, and the reintegration of those demobilized forces back into the economic and social life of their societies. Successful programs are characterized by the integration of the political, military, humanitarian, informational, developmental, and financial management areas. The PO force has a key role in supporting

these programs. Primarily, it must provide a secure environment. If the population does not perceive that they can conduct their daily affairs in a secure environment, they will not support disarmament or demobilization. Civil agencies have the lead and should be responsible for the economic and developmental assistance, the political negotiations, the fiscal support, the social programs and the policy support. Military support could consist of:

(a) Providing and maintaining a safe and secure environment.

(b) Supporting arms embargoes.

(c) Observing and verifying disarmament by site and unit inspections.

(d) Providing continuous intelligence, constant surveillance, and flexible reconnaissance.

(e) Safety and security of storage sites.

(f) EOD assistance for destruction.

(g) Logistic assistance in disposition of weapons and ordnance.

(h) Technical expertise on military ordnance.

(i) IO.

(j) Controlling and securing assembly of units and equipment.

(k) Location of arms caches.

(l) Support for civilian general weapons management programs by providing a security environment in which UN CIVPOL and HN police can operate.

(m) Providing training assistance to newly formed military units.

(11) Demining. The US military clears mines for mobility during operations however, humanitarian demining is a key part of the disarmament process and is ultimately a HN responsibility. US forces do not physically detect, lift, or destroy landmines in these cases; however they assist in training others in demining techniques and procedures. IGOs and private commercial companies that specialize in the eradication of these devices conduct the majority of worldwide humanitarian demining.

(12) Decontamination. The US military may assist a HN with a potentially long-term effort to eliminate the residual hazards from the use of CBRN weapons, materials or agents. EOD skills may be required to handle residual CBRN devices discovered during decontamination tasks.

For further guidance on decontamination refer to consequence management in JP 3-40, Combating Weapons of Mass Destruction.

(13) Seize, secure, control and destroy CBRN. The US military seizes CBRN weapons, materials, agents, means of delivery and related infrastructure and expertise during military operations for destruction or redirection as appropriate. These activities may be conducted in a non-permissive environment, as well as in a post-conflict permissive environment. Long-term elimination and redirection tasks may be transferred from the US military to another US agency, or other agencies as directed.

For further guidance on eliminating CBRN refer to the Handbook for Joint Weapons of Mass Destruction (WMD) Elimination Operations.

(14) Reducing the Threat of Weapons of Mass Destruction (WMD). The US military may be involved with helping a state to enhance the physical security; emplace detection equipment; and reduce, dismantle or redirect their WMD programs. Threat reduction activities should be conducted in a post-conflict (i.e., permissive environment).

b. **Humanitarian Assistance and Social Well-being.** This sector includes programs conducted to relieve or reduce the results of natural or man-made disasters or other endemic conditions such as human suffering, disease, or privation that might represent a serious threat to life, or that can result in great damage to or loss of property. The goal of this mission sector is to provide for emergency humanitarian needs, establish a foundation for development, and institutionalize long-term development programs. The assistance provided is designed to supplement or complement the efforts of the HN civil authorities and various IGOs and NGOs that may have the primary responsibility for providing HA. The need to establish a secure environment, ensure the survival of the population, and maintain a minimum level of economic activity in a region may require that military units participate in public service tasks during the emergency phase of the operation until such time that NGOs, IGOs, and HN capacity is established.

For further guidance on FHA, refer to JP 3-29, Foreign Humanitarian Assistance.

c. **Justice and Reconciliation**

(1) This section concerns establishing public order and safety and providing for social reconciliation. The objective is that the country will establish a self-sustaining public law and order system in accordance with internationally recognized standards with respect for human rights and freedoms, operated inside a safe and secure environment that initially might have to be established by the PO force. Civilian organizations have the primary responsibility to work with the HN to train, advise, and support their efforts to establish a viable rule of law system and facilitate social recovery. However, the PO force may be required to provide limited and focused support during the emergency phase until such time that civilian capacity can be developed. The following are general considerations for the PO force commander supporting rule of law:

(a) Include rule of law and public security issues in intelligence preparation. This should include obtaining information from specialists on transnational crime and criminology in general, as well as political specialists and sociologists who can analyze the strengths and weakness of the existing system.

(b) Establish coordination and information sharing mechanisms, such as fusion cells, to integrate intelligence from deployed military units, special gendarmerie type units, special police units, US and/or UN CIVPOL trainers, Department of Justice (DOJ) advisors, HN institutions, security contractors and other public security organizations.

(c) Understand legal constraints and restraints and request clarification as necessary.

(2) The rule of law consists of three related fields: police, judicial, and penal.

(a) Police

<u>1.</u> To assist in meeting police obligations, the HN may request that the UN or a specific country establish a CIVPOL assistance mission to assist them in community policing. CIVPOL responsibilities encompass a wide range of activities that can be broadly categorized as follows: advising and reporting; reforming and restructure of local police services; training, mentoring, skills transfer, and policy capability enhancement; and performing executive law enforcement functions as authorized. However, when the indigenous security and police forces are nonexistent, incapable, or obstructionist and the CIVPOL cannot generate sufficient capacity quickly enough, the PO force may assist in establishing public order. The PO force has limits because it possesses neither the capacity nor the capability for community policing. The CIVPOL will be a separate component of the PO mission. The PO force must work closely with the CIVPOL and both must understand each others' exact authority. The PO force commander may require addition of police type units (not a US capability). Their mission includes deterring civil disturbances, riot control, and collection and analysis of criminal intelligence. Special police units to participate in high-risk arrests or close protection of very important persons and election candidates may be required. The following are guidelines for combined military and police PO:

<u>a.</u> Understand the ROE/rules for the use of force.

<u>b.</u> Allow the HN or CIVPOL to handle situations involving local nationals as much as possible. In a crisis, the military can detain suspected criminals pending the arrival of the arrest authority.

<u>c.</u> Ensure the PO force is aware of the cultural traditions and standards of the HN. The PO force should be respectful and supportive of the HN law enforcements agents.

<u>d.</u> Establish close coordination and information sharing with police authorities especially concerning rules of evidence and the objectives of the enforcement policy.

2. PO force support to police authority could consist of:

a. Providing a safe and secure environment so that police can function.

b. Safeguarding institutions of government and key officials.

c. Providing military advisors and trainers to police as required and authorized.

d. Detaining war criminals and supporting authorized authorities conducting high-risk arrests.

e. Conducting combined security patrols with police.

f. Supporting police presence and search patrols.

g. Controlling crowds, riots, and urban unrest.

h. Detaining suspected criminals.

i. Enforcing curfews.

j. Facilitating freedom of movement.

k. Providing intelligence.

l. Preventing looting and pilferage.

m. Securing key facilities and cultural properties.

n. Providing limited logistic and transportation support.

o. Deterring violent acts.

p. Supporting with IO.

q. Security of emergency services, security of IGOs/NGOs, and security of vital infrastructure.

(b) Judicial. The US DOJ along with the DOS and the IGOs will lead the efforts to build judicial capability and capacity. The PO force may assist in the establishment of a workable judicial system with judge advocate and CA functional specialty support. The legal standards, and their effect on SOFA and MOUs, are important considerations. The JFC should engage functional specialty advisors in the development of systems to ensure that military concerns are addressed. Until the HN judicial system is functional, international courts and tribunals may be responsible for post-conflict justice.

(c) Penal. The HN in concert with international advisors should establish standards and rules of confinement when establishing a working penal system in accordance with applicable international instruments, norms, and standards. Although IGOs may assume the responsibility to assist in training HN personnel in detention operations, the PO force may have to support such activity by designing and conducting training packages, providing technical advice, and supporting the development of institutional capacity operationally and administratively. In emergency situations, the PO force commander may establish and run temporary confinement facilities until civilian agencies generate sufficient capability and capacity. The contingent forces should be prepared to deal with the temporary confinement of civilian prisoners accused of civil crimes. Considerations should be given to deployment of the appropriate occupational specialties for confinement duties.

(d) Applicable Law. Agreement among the parties as to the applicable law is a key step in establishing rule of law. IGOs and advisors from the PO force must review and assist in the development of a penal code to ensure its conformity with appropriate minimum international standards. There may be a period of time where the applicable law is in flux and commanders and administrators at all levels must remain flexible.

(3) Reconciliation. PO are conducted in situations where there have been human rights abuses and social trauma to include the appropriation of lands and property. The process of seeking justice through legal procedures may be more important in building respect for the rule of law than in the meting out of summary justice. The tasks of promoting justice, psychological relief, and reconciliation are challenging and time consuming, but the end goal of achieving reconciliation will lead to a sustainable peace. PO force support could consist of:

(a) Supporting resettlement and land reform to allow safe passage and safe return.

(b) Providing intelligence concerning missing persons, detainees, and human rights violations.

(c) Supporting reconciliation mechanisms if they are established.

(d) Monitoring human rights in the new security organizations and providing human rights training for new defense structures.

(e) Reporting human rights violations and working to prevent further abuse.

(f) Protecting social, civil, and cultural rights within the limits of the mandate.

d. **Governance and Participation.** The establishment of governance and a workable administration leading to a civil society is the responsibility of the HN. However, the PO force must be prepared in the short run to establish a military government if warranted, or to provide short-term support to an established HN government or interim government sponsored by the UN or other IGO. The main goal for the military is to create an environment conducive to stable governance. Civil agencies will reestablish the administrative framework, support national constituting processes, support political reform, and establish/reestablish civil society. Military efforts could consist of:

(1) Supporting civil administration.

(2) Supporting elections.

(3) Fostering the establishment of effective interim or transitional government.

(4) Supporting public education in the development of civil society.

(5) Fostering the establishment of free and open media sources.

e. **Economic Stabilization and Infrastructure Mission**

(1) Civilian agencies have the lead responsibility for this mission sector but the PO force may render support during the emergency phase of infrastructure restoration. Infrastructure restoration consists of the reconstitution of power, transportation, communications, health and sanitation, fire fighting, education system, mortuary services, and environmental control. This must include restoring the functioning of economic production and distribution. In addition to the overarching requirements to ensure a secure environment, PO force support to infrastructure restoration could consist of:

(a) Providing emergency reestablishment of critical infrastructure (basic services such as transportation system and health systems) to prevent loss of life and the spread of instability.

(b) Providing advice to civilian agencies.

(2) Economic stabilization consists of restoring employment opportunities, initiating market reform, mobilizing domestic and foreign investment, supervising monetary reform, and rebuilding public structures. This should be a pure civil responsibility, supported by the military, with numerous IGOs, NGOs, and other implementation agencies involved. Agencies such as the World Bank provide financial management and technical assistance to economically depressed countries through its International Development Association to bolster economic growth and improve living conditions. However, the military, particularly CA functional specialty teams, must be prepared to undertake responsibility for tasks in this area in the absence of civilian agencies, especially early in PO.

f. **Public Diplomacy and Information Operations.** This critical mission overlaps all five of the previously outlined mission sectors. Public diplomacy actions are civilian agency efforts to promote an understanding of the reconstruction efforts, rule of law, and civic responsibility through PA and international public diplomacy operations. Its objective is to promote and sustain consent for PB both within the HN and externally in the region and in the larger international community. Civil agencies conduct educational and cultural exchanges, information activities, local training and education of indigenous media, and assist in developing the local information infrastructure.

5. Peace Building Personnel and Peace Operations Forces

PO forces have key roles in supporting PB. Service capabilities that provide needed advice, assistance, coordination, and functional expertise include US Army CA units, United States Marine Corps CA groups, United States Air Force support to CA, engineering, HSS, MP/SF, PSYOP, religious ministry support, transportation, and the USCG. Commanders cannot rely solely on their CA personnel in large-scale PO, due to their limited capacity. PO forces assigned to PB mission sectors must be prepared to perform traditional CA functions, which may require that commanders seek out individual subject matter experts in the various mission sectors.

6. Command and Control for Peace Building

In PO (generally), and PB (in particular), civilian organizations have the responsibility and the lead. Therefore, C2, or rather the harmonization among the various civil entities and the military must be clearly understood and coordinated. To achieve a holistic approach to PB requires communications and understanding among the various centers, commissions, staffs, augmentations, field offices, and agencies. Complicating these efforts are varying national perspectives regarding the mandate and the resulting mission interpretation. Whereas the US could interpret the mission in terms of FP, liaison, and limited direct support, another country could view the same mandate in terms of strict neutrality and mediation or one of observation, interposition, and transition assistance. Additionally, there will be various interpretations of operational environment among the military, HN, NGOs, IGOs, OGAs, IPI, and others. The military must understand all of these positions and maintain lines of communications to resolve issues as they arise. The commander may use various mechanisms to assist him in this endeavor, one of which is the CMOC.

a. **Lead Agency.** In UN sponsored PO, the UNSG may appoint (based on a Security Council mandate) a SRSG. The SRSG is the UNSG's representative to the government of the HN. The SRSG will be the overall coordinator of the UN sponsored PO. In some PO, the military may be the lead agency and be required to assume full control of a HN for a period. In this case, a military government may be formed and the country placed under martial law.

b. **Parallel.** In PO, where the PO force is supplied by a lead nation or alliance, civil-military coordination and military C2 will be vested in parallel structures. Integration and synchronization of efforts will be achieved through LNOs, military staff augmentation to civilian agencies, CMOCs, CIMIC centers, UN information centers, joint civil commissions, or other such coordination bodies established for that purpose.

7. Peace Building Planning Considerations

The planning for PB should be integrated into the overall planning for PO or the "stabilize" and "enable civil authority" phase of the major operation and should begin as early as possible. Planning begins with the receipt of the missions followed by a comprehensive mission analysis. Planning should be conducted in a collaborative manner with the civilian and HN agencies that have the ultimate responsibility for the PB. PB planning considerations are discussed below.

a. **Civil/Military Synchronization.** PO force commanders should develop a synchronization process. Objectives and desired/undesired effects should be determined among civil-military partners for each line of operation and linked to overall diplomatic, information, military, and economic considerations.

b. **Military End State and the Termination Criteria.** Because the national strategic end state may be general or broad in nature, it may be difficult to determine whether military operations should be terminated. A requirement, therefore, exists, to determine the military end state and the termination criteria. The military end state is the set of required conditions that defines achievement of all military objectives. It normally represents a point in time and/or circumstances beyond which the President does not require the military instrument of national power as the primary means to achieve remaining national objectives. They establish benchmarks that can prompt a transition from military to civil effort. The termination criteria, on the other hand, describe the relevant and measurable standards that must be met before a joint operation can be concluded. The actual success of military operations will be measured against the national strategic end state and not just attainment of the military end state. The termination criteria should be developed through a collaborative planning process with both military and civilian agencies. They should relate to the national strategic as well as the military end state and the local and cultural realities of the HN.

c. **Intelligence**

(1) Intelligence must adapt to support those special needs for PB. Political, economic, linguistic, ethnic, and other factors influence populations and determine the "people" relevance to the mission. Consider the following as some of the possible intelligence sources for PB:

(a) UN and its organizations as well as various CA units, PSYOP teams, and NGOs may have been in the area for many years and may have area studies, country studies, and other useful resources.

(b) Patterns of criminal activity.

(c) Economic conditions.

(d) Environmental concerns.

(e) Threats to vulnerable populations (women, children, aged).

(f) Police and paramilitary forces.

(g) Cultural and religious factors.

(h) Agricultural patterns.

(i) The military and political context of the region bordering the operational area, such as police, paramilitary forces, terrorist groups, and organizations operating in the operational area.

(2) Creativity in establishing nonthreatening information-sharing relationships with NGOs can assist a commander in developing his operational picture.

d. **Financial Management**

(1) The PO force commander should determine the authority to provide or receive multinational support. There will be many nontraditional requirements that must be met. The PO force commander should determine what additional financial management support will be needed for peace related programs. Legal authorities and sources of money may have to be requested. Procedures should be developed to coordinate the disbursement of funds.

(2) Several mechanisms and funding authorities have been granted to GCCs to be used to respond to urgent humanitarian relief and reconstruction requirements within their areas of responsibility, by carrying out programs that will immediately assist the indigenous people and support PB.

e. **Logistics**

(1) During PB, logistic planning includes support for the overwhelming demands for food, water, billeting, waste disposal, movement control, environmental, and safety concerns. HN needs for supplies and services may increase substantially above the PO forces' own requirements. The magnitude of the FHA effort, the status of the HN's infrastructure, and the requirements of the peace implementation agreement are factors. Contractors can provide a range of support, expertise, and assistance to the PO force and civilian agencies.

(2) The logistic support plan should identify multinational PO force support as well as anticipated NGOs and IGOs requirements. The plan should identify what areas will come under multinational control, US unilateral control, and what areas will remain under HN control. The lead nation for each logistic concern must be identified. The logistic plan should address specific agreements, such as environmental cleanup requirements, exemption from customs duties, HAZMAT storage, and transit restrictions.

(3) The logistics staff office should inform the PO force commander on the impact of the PO force on the local economy. The PO force commander should, in coordination with the civil authority, develop policies to reduce these impacts.

(4) Limited availability of movement and transport resources will require planning, coordination, and cooperation among all military and civil participants.

(5) Public health will be of key concern and the provisioning of water, food, HSS, fuel, and shelter must be considered in coordination with the humanitarian agencies.

f. **Transition to Civil Authority.** The relationships established in the initial stages of the PO, coupled with accurate assessments of progress achieved in civil-military implementation, are crucial to affecting a smooth transition to civil authority. The PO force commander should conduct collaborative planning as early as possible to include the MNF, OGAs and IGOs, the HN if possible, and NGOs as appropriate. The transition plan should rest on a complete understanding of the capabilities, responsibilities, and resources of all participants. The result should be an agreed plan, including MOE and resources, which results in decreasing military involvement and increasing civil involvement. Transitions can occur at different times in the PO and in different parts of the HN. The PO force commander, in synchronization with civil agencies must manage these transition events.

g. **PSYOP.** Well-conceived, clearly stated, and thoroughly disseminated PSYOP can make the difference between success and failure in PB. The fundamentals of transparency and legitimacy demand that the PO force commander engage openly within this complex environment. PSYOP are essential to gain the support of the HN in reconstructing infrastructure, establishing governance, and reestablishing civil society.

h. **Legal.** PB involves a myriad of statutory, regulatory, and police considerations, both foreign and domestic. In some instances, conflicting laws may be involved. Commanders at all levels will become involved with local governments and civil authorities. They should anticipate negotiating with local leaders and factions in order to accomplish the mission.

8. **Peace Building Employment Phases**

The PO force conducts PB in three phases. These phases may not be sequential but may occur simultaneously in various parts of the country depending on local circumstances.

a. Early in the **emergency phase** of PB, critical and immediate tasks normally accomplished by civilian organizations temporarily exceed their capabilities. Note: "Temporarily" could be months or years in duration. The PO force should perform those tasks or cooperate to ensure that they are accomplished. The PO force should provide immediate relief to save lives and sustain critical infrastructure and provide a secure environment to preempt criminal elements and spoilers from gaining control over areas of the country.

b. In the **stabilization phase** civil organizations have generated sufficient capability and capacity for the PO force to shift toward facilitating civil implementation.

c. In the **normalization phase** the PO force transfers all of the PB tasks to civil organizations or the HN and resumes the standard peacetime relationship with the country.

For detailed descriptions of tasks and considerations in each mission sector across employment phases (alternatively described as "Initial Response," "Transformation," and "Fostering Sustainability"), see Post-Conflict Reconstruction Essential Tasks *of the State Department's Office of the Coordinator for Reconstruction and Stabilization, available at http://www.state.gov/ s/crs/rls/52959.htm. For another detailed task list, see the UN's* An Inventory of Post-Conflict Peace-Building Activities, *available at http://www.un.org/esa/peacebuilding/Library/ st_esa_246.pdf.*

APPENDIX A
UNITED NATIONS INVOLVEMENT IN PEACE OPERATIONS

1. **General**

a. **The meaning of the terms "peacekeeping" and "peacekeeper" as used by the UN differ from the meanings used in both US joint doctrine and Allied joint doctrine**. The UN uses "peacekeeping" to identify what the US would term "peace operations" and an Allied joint publication (AJP) would term "peace support operations." In this JP and this appendix, for clarity, the US terms are used except where specifically noted as "UN peacekeeping" or "UN peacekeepers."

b. The primary responsibility of the UN is the maintenance of international peace and security. The UN Charter provides the TOR for the various elements of the UN in fulfilling this responsibility. Article 29 of the UN Charter is generally agreed to be the basis of authority for the UN to conduct PKO. Article 42 of the UN Charter provides the authority for PEO.

c. Historical

(1) UN peacekeeping was developed as a series of ad hoc practical mechanisms used by the UN to help contain armed conflicts and settle them by peaceful means. The mechanism devised by the UN to ensure international peace and security is outlined in Chapters VI, VII, and VIII of the UN Charter. During the Cold War, the UN conducted what was called traditional UN peacekeeping missions. These missions were primarily political operations supported by the military and dependent upon the consent and cooperation of the belligerents. They were usually restricted to the interposition of unarmed observers or lightly armed UN peacekeepers between warring states once the following conditions had been met:

(a) A cease fire agreement was in place.

(b) The parties to the conflict fully consented to their deployment.

(2) The objectives of traditional "UN peacekeeping" were generally limited simply to reporting conditions following the political agreement.

(3) These UN peacekeeping activities now referred to as "integrated missions" by the UN, may be authorized under UN Charter, Chapters VI and VII are multifunctional missions, in which the military component is only one part of a comprehensive political, diplomatic, humanitarian, and economic effort. Their military objectives include supporting OGAs, IGOs, and NGOs in the provision of humanitarian aid, the organization and protection of elections, the supervision of government functions, the disarmament and demobilization of a large number of parties, the repatriation and rehabilitation of refugees, the protection of safe areas, restoration of national government and institutions, and other tasks. The environment of a complex integrated mission is considerably more bellicose and complex than that of the traditional UN peacekeeping,

and is characterized largely by unstable intrastate conflicts and is often hostile as a virtual state of war existed or is in temporary remission.

2. United Nations Headquarters Organization

a. The Under Secretary Generals (USYGs) are responsible to the UNSG for policy concerns with respect to "UN peacekeeping" operations.

b. The USYG for Peacekeeping is responsible to the UNSG for the day-to-day operational matters affecting PO. United Nations Department for Peacekeeping Operations (UNDPKO) also provides management oversight for several missions under the Department of Political Affairs. Under the USYG for Peacekeeping is the military advisor to the UNSG as well as the Director of the Office of Mission Support (OMS), who is responsible for financial management, personnel management, and logistic support of PO.

c. The Department of Peacekeeping Operations (DPKO) is the operational arm for all UN peacekeeping, and is responsible for the conduct, management, direction, planning, and preparation of those operations. It develops plans and methodologies for UN peacekeeping (Office of Operations, Military Division and Civil Police Division).

3. Subordinate United Nations Organizations

UN organizations primarily concerned with PO include the following:

a. **United Nations Office of the High Commissioner for Refugees (UNHCR).** The UNHCR has a major role in coordinating aid to refugees, returnees, and displaced persons. Coordination with the UNHCR is critical for any humanitarian relief effort. Failure to coordinate with UNHCR before and during the operation, or failure to meet UNHCR standards, may preclude the UNHCR from accepting transfer of equipment, supplies, and facilities as the military disengages. To preclude this, a working relationship should be established with UNHCR immediately upon notification of a mission with UNHCR.

b. **United Nations Office for the Coordination of Humanitarian Affairs.** OCHA's mission is to mobilize and coordinate effective and principled humanitarian action in partnership with national and international actors.

c. **United Nations Disaster Management Team (UN-DMT).** The appointed UN resident coordinator has a crucial role in providing leadership to the UN team at country level, and also coordinates locally represented NGOs as required. The resident coordinator convenes the UN-DMT at country level, seeking unity of effort among all various NGOs and IGOs. The UN-DMT is the primary agency responsible for coordinating assistance to persons compelled to leave their homes as a result of disasters, natural and otherwise.

d. **United Nations Development Programme (UNDP).** UNDP promotes the incorporation of disaster mitigation in development planning and funds technical assistance for all aspects of disaster management. Work is long range.

e. **World Food Programme (WFP).** WFP is an operational, relief-oriented organization. It provides targeted food aid and supports rehabilitation, reconstruction, and risk-reducing development programs. Targeted food aid is special subsistence aligned to a special segment of the population.

f. **United Nations Children's Fund (UNICEF).** UNICEF is a relief-oriented organization which attends to the well-being of children and women, especially child health and nutrition.

g. **World Health Organization (WHO).** WHO is primarily involved in long-range programs. It provides advice and assistance in all aspects of preventive and curative health care.

h. **Food and Agriculture Organization (FAO).** FAO is an organization also involved in long-range programs. It provides technical advice in reducing vulnerability and helps in the rehabilitation of agriculture, livestock, and fisheries.

4. **Planning Process**

DPKO is responsible for developing strategic estimates, operational plans, force requirements, guidance for the UN PO force commander, guidelines for the troop contributing country, and ROE. DPKO uses an integrated planning process very similar in purpose to the US interagency process. The plans, objectives, and resource requirements of the various UN mission components (political, military, logistic, administrative, civil police, humanitarian, DDRRR, gender awareness, safety and security, mine awareness, electoral support, etc.) are coordinated and synchronized to achieve optimal efficiency and effectiveness. The lack of a standing mission headquarters staff makes detailed planning and initial execution a challenge. DPKO is also responsible for the training and establishment of all new mission headquarters. This requirement is accomplished by deployment of a transition team composed of representatives from the various mission components.

a. **Plan Development.** Based on the direction the UNSG receives from the UNSC, the final plan will be developed based on existing arrangements and the informal negotiations with member states during the PO force generation phase. Nations will be formally requested to contribute MILOBs, staff officers, and formed contingents to a UN force. The CIVPOL Division is responsible for the generation of CIVPOL resources.

b. **Establishing the PO Force Commander and Headquarters.** Upon the approval of the mandate and the budget plan, the UNSG will ensure that negotiations are commenced with the disputing parties and the HN for preparation of the SOFA. The UNSG, with the approval of the UNSC, appoints the head of PO in a mission area. He/she determines the further delegation of authority in the field on behalf of the UNSG. The chief of the military component in UN peacekeeping (the PO force commander or chief MILOB) is appointed by the UNSG and given appropriate authority over all military units and personnel in the mission area in the light of operational requirements. A SRSG supported by political and mediation staff, conducts diplomatic efforts to resolve the conflict.

c. **Participating Member-State Preparations.** Participating member states will negotiate the extent of their contribution to the PO with the UN through a MOU. It is not unusual for the UN to place limits on national contributions due to nonmilitary factors such as financial limitations.

d. **Reception and Service Support.** The OMS will usually deploy an advance party to establish reception and service support arrangements for the operation. The UN will plan, organize, and direct the deployment of the PO force to the theater.

e. **Operational Control.** The operational chain of command for PO will be from the unit commander to the PO force commander to the HOM, usually the SRSG. In certain cases, the US forces may be placed under OPCON of a foreign commander, but combatant command (command authority) is exercised only in the US chain of command.

5. **United Nations Documents**

a. **United Nations Mandate.** The mandate and the mission are central to all PO. It's a document that comes directly from the UNSCRs. It will normally be quite specific as to the tasks to be undertaken and will translate readily in missions to each component of the mission.

b. **UN Secretary-General Directive.** The UNSG, upon appointing the PO force commander, will issue a formal written directive outlining the TOR.

c. **PO Force Commander's Directive.** This is also referred to as an SOP or PO force standing order. Upon receipt of the Force Commander's Directive from DPKO, the PO force commander will prepare more detailed regulations and operating procedures that will be issued to the PO force.

d. **UN Rules of Engagement.** The UN master list of numbered ROE provides the rules from which specific ROE for future PO should be drawn. The master list is intended to cover the broad spectrum of requirements for any UN PO.

APPENDIX B
COMMAND RELATIONSHIPS

1. The following figures (B-1, B-2, and B-3) are extracted from the UN Standard Training Module and depict the possible UN chain of command and UN peacekeeping organizational structures a US commander may encounter. Nations will rarely, if ever, relinquish national command of their forces. As such, forces participating in a multinational PO will always have at least two distinct chains of command: a national chain of command and a multinational chain of

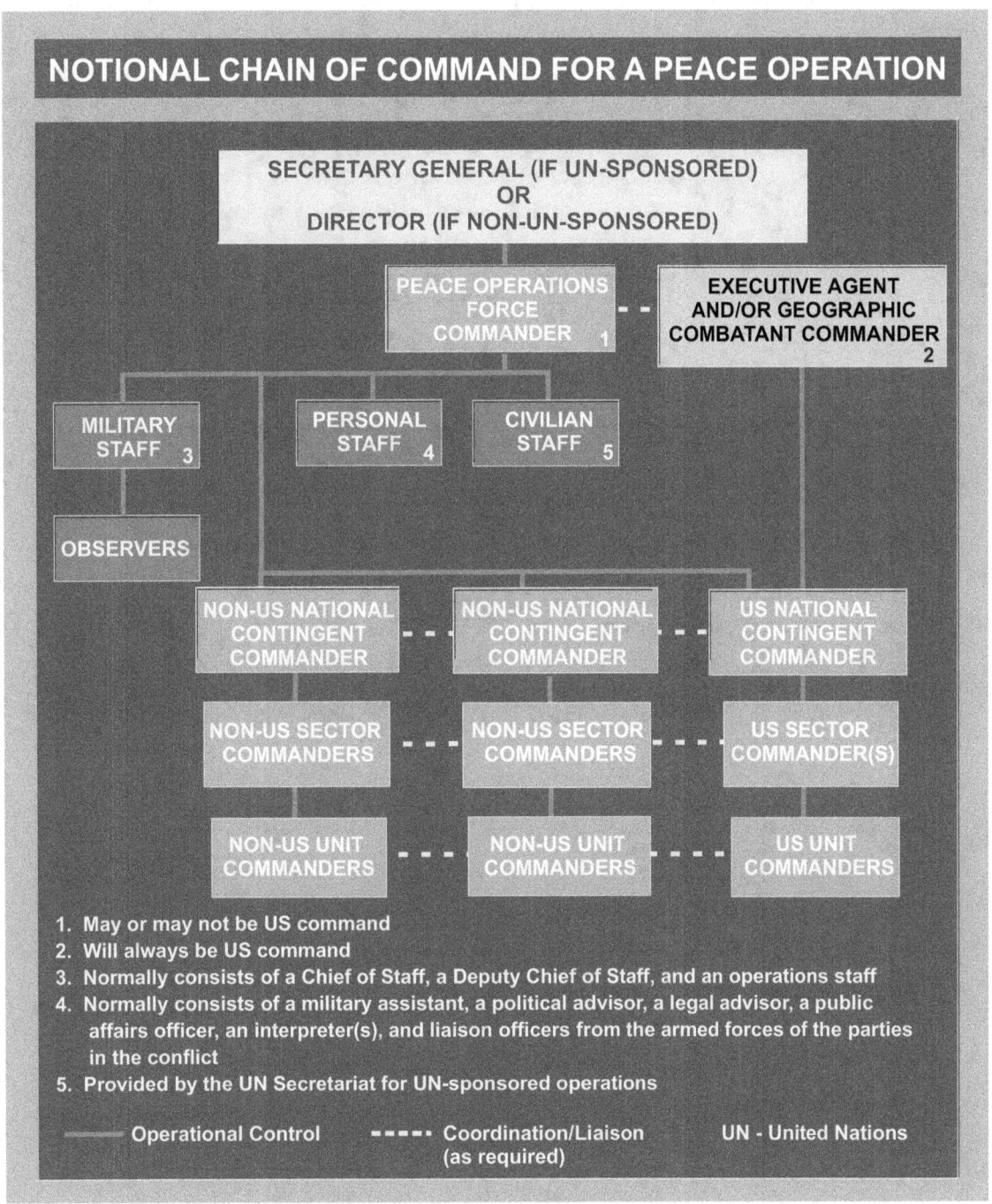

Figure B-1. Notional Chain of Command for a Peace Operation

command. Although in certain circumstances US forces may be placed under the OPCON of non-US commanders, the US chain of command will remain inviolate, running from the President to the supported JFC.

2. Traditional "UN peacekeeping" operations normally have as their main element a military component. CIVPOL may be present and all are supported by a civilian administration component. These PO tend to maintain their structure and organization with only minor changes for the duration of the mandate. The UN Military Observer Group in India and Pakistan; UN Mission in Ethiopia and Eritrea; and UN Forces in Cyprus are examples of traditional UN peacekeeping organizations.

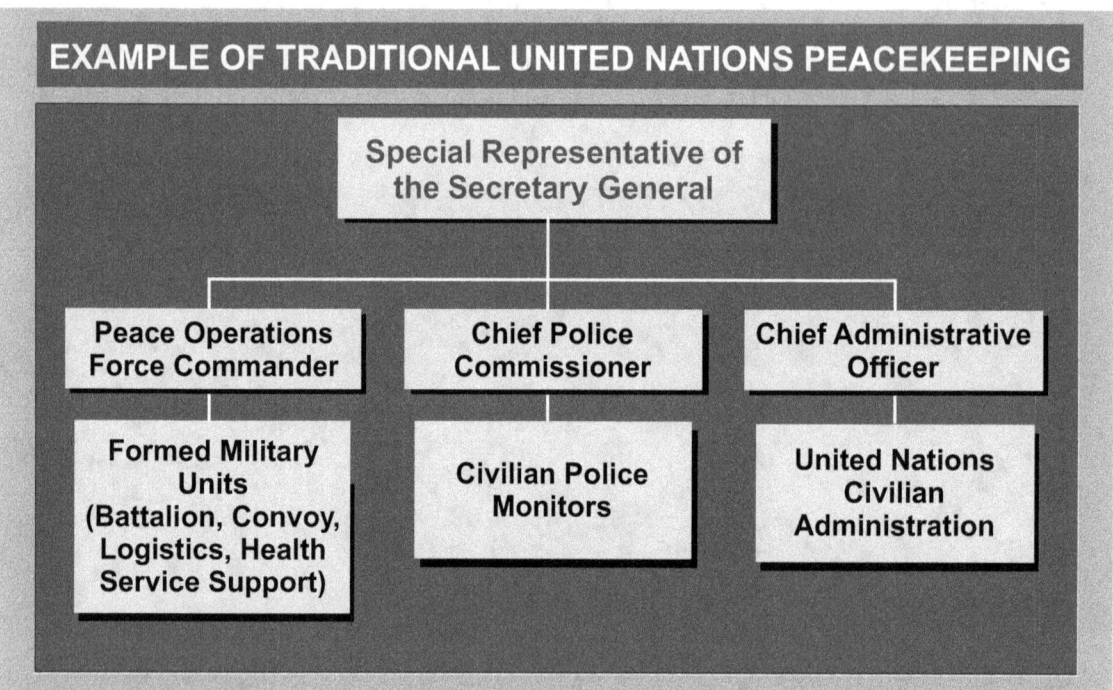

Figure B-2. Example of Traditional United Nations Peacekeeping

3. Complex "UN peacekeeping," by definition involve situations that require the participation of the full scope of the elements of the UN family of organizations. The military and CIVPOL components, however important in size, normally are just specialized elements supporting the mandate with their specific capabilities. The HA, the civil administration, the public information components among many others, are supporting the success of the peace efforts with their own capabilities. Thus, these elements have larger organizations and resources than in traditional peacekeeping. The situations tend to be more fluid and difficult to predict, imposing continuous reassessments of the mandate. Reorganization and redeployment are normal in these operations. The first mission to be described as complex was the successful UN Transition Authority in Cambodia. Current examples of these are the UN Transitional Administration in East Timor that was succeeded by the UN Mission of Support in East Timor, UN Mission in Sierra Leone, and the UN Mission in the Democratic Republic of Congo (see Figure B-3).

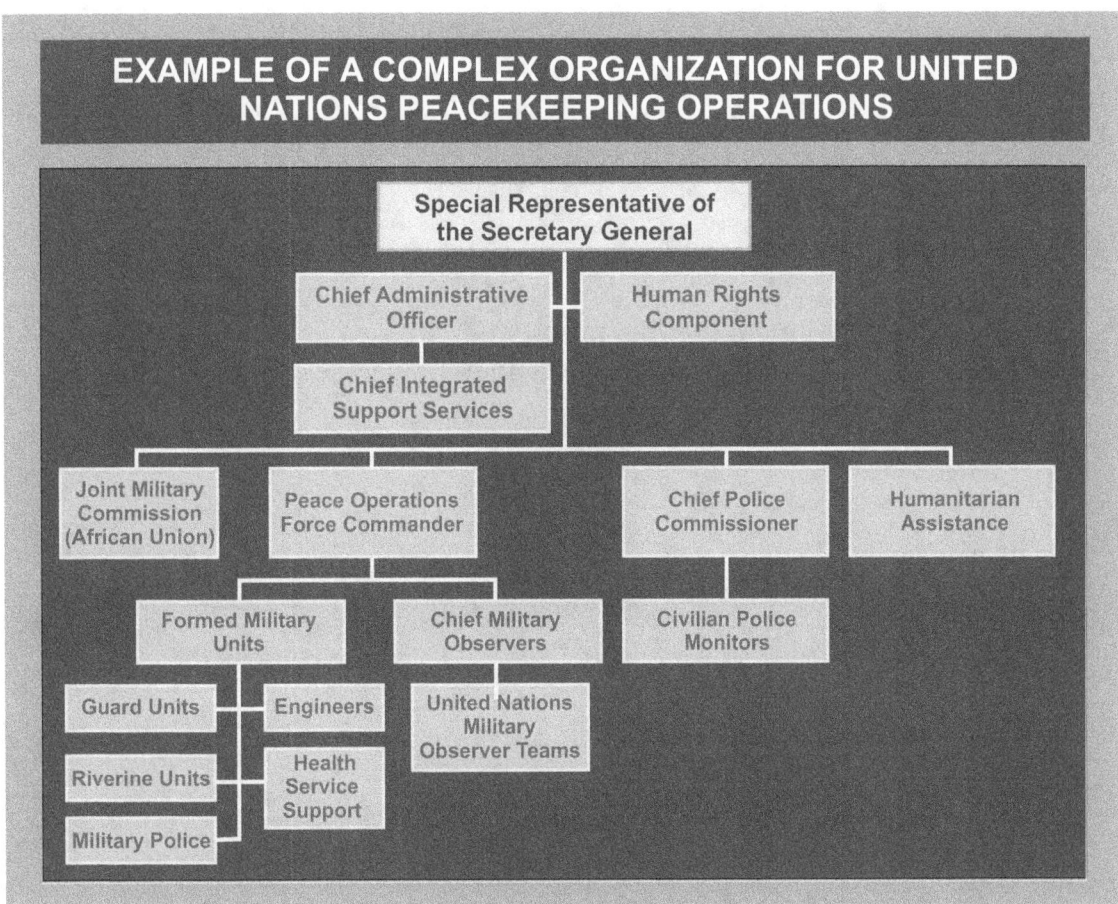

Figure B-3. Example of a Complex Organization for United Nations Peacekeeping Operations

Intentionally Blank

APPENDIX C
REFERENCES

The development of JP 3-07.3 is based upon the following primary references.

1. **Strategy and Policy Documents**

   a. *UN Participation Act* of 1945 as amended (PL 79-264).

   b. *UN Charter.*

   c. North Atlantic Treaty.

   d. Boutros Boutros-Ghali, *An Agenda For Peace: Preventative Diplomacy, Peacemaking, and Peacekeeping,* Report of the Secretary-General, 1992.

   e. Boutros Boutros-Ghali, *Supplement to An Agenda For Peace: Position Paper of the Secretary-General* on the Occasion of the Fiftieth Anniversary of the United Nations, 1995.

   f. Brahimi Report – Lakhdar Brahimi, Chairman of the *Panel on United Nations Peace Operations* – Report to the General Assembly and Security Council, 21 August 2000.

   g. Executive Order 10206, *Providing for Support of United Nations' Activities Directed to the Peaceful Settlement of Disputes.*

   h. *The Foreign Assistance Act* of 1961 as amended (PL 87-195), Part II, Chapter 6.

   i. *Title 10, United States Code.*

   j. *National Defense Strategy.*

   k. *National Military Strategy.*

   l. *National Military Strategy to Combat Weapons of Mass Destruction.*

   m. *National Security Strategy.*

   n. National Disclosure Policy-1, *National Policy and Procedures for the Disclosure of Classified Military Information to Foreign Governments and International Organizations.*

   o. Presidential Decision Directive 25, *United States: Clinton Administration Policy on Reforming Multilateral Peace Operations.*

   p. CJCSI 3121.01B, *Standing Rules of Engagement/Standing Rules for the Use of Force for US Forces.*

q. CJCS Handbook 5260, *Commander's Handbook for Antiterrorism Awareness*.

r. DODD 2065.1E, *Assignment of Personnel to United Nations Missions*.

s. DODD 3000.3, *Policy for Nonlethal Weapons*.

2. **Joint Publications**

a. JP 1, *Doctrine for the Armed Forces of the United States*.

b. JP 1-0, *Personnel Support for Joint Operations*.

c. JP 1-02, *DOD Dictionary of Military and Associated Terms*.

d. JP 2-0, *Joint Intelligence*.

e. JP 2-01, *Joint and National Intelligence Support to Military Operations*.

f. JP 2-01.3, *Joint Intelligence Preparation of the Operational Environment*.

g. JP 3-0, *Joint Operations*.

h. JP 3-05, *Doctrine for Joint Special Operations*.

i. JP 3-07.1, *Joint Tactics, Techniques, and Procedures for Foreign Internal Defense (FID)*.

j. JP 3-07.2, *Antiterrorism*.

k. JP 3-08, *Interagency, Intergovernmental Organization, and Nongovernmental Organization Coordination During Joint Operations, Vols I and II*.

l. JP 3-09, *Joint Fire Support*.

m. JP 3-13.3, *Operations Security*.

n. JP 3-16, *Multinational Operations*.

o. JP 3-18, *Joint Doctrine for Forcible Entry Operations*.

p. JP 3-33, *Joint Task Force Headquarters*.

q. JP 3-34, *Joint Engineer Operations*.

r. JP 3-40, *Joint Doctrine for Combating Weapons of Mass Destruction*.

s. *Handbook for Joint Weapons of Mass Destruction (WMD) Elimination Operations.*

t. JP 3-53, *Joint Doctrine for Psychological Operations.*

u. JP 3-57, *Civil-Military Operations.*

v. JP 3-61, *Public Affairs.*

w. JP 4-0, *Doctrine for Logistic Support of Joint Operations.*

x. JP 4-01, *Joint Doctrine for the Defense Transportation System.*

y. JP 4-01.2, *Sealift Support to Joint Operations.*

z. JP 4-01.5, *Joint Tactics, Techniques, and Procedures for Transportation Terminal Operations.*

aa. JP 4-02, *Health Service Support.*

bb. JP 5-0, *Joint Operation Planning.*

cc. Joint Warfighting Center, *Joint Task Force Commander's Handbook for Peace Operations.*

dd. CJCS Guide 5260, *Antiterrorism Personal Protection Guide, A Self-Help Guide to Antiterrorism.*

ee. United States Joint Forces Command Joint Warfighting Center, Joint Doctrine Series, Pamphlet 2, *Doctrinal Implications of Low Collateral Damage Capabilities.*

3. **Multi-Service Publications**

a. FM 3-22.40, Naval Tactics, Techniques, and Procedures 3-07.3.2, MCWP 315.8, AFTTP(I) 3-2.45, USCG Pub 3-07.31, *NLW, Tactical Employment of Nonlethal Weapons.*

b. FM 3-07.31, MCWP 3-33.8, AFTTP(I) 3-2.40, *Multi-Service Tactics, Techniques, and Procedures for Conducting Peace Operations.*

4. **Multinational Publications**

a. Canada, B-GJ-005-307/FP-030, *Peace Support Operations.*

b. United Kingdom, Joint Warfare Publication 3-50, *The Military Contribution to Peace Support Operations.*

c. AJP 3.4.1, *Peace Support Operations*.

d. Allied Tactical Publication 3.4.1.1, *Peace Support Operations Techniques and Procedures*.

5. **Service Publications**

a. FM 3-07 (FM 100-20), *Stability Operations and Support Operations*.

b. FM 100-23, *Peace Operations*.

6. **Internet Sites**

a. Joint Doctrine Joint Electronic Library: http://www.dtic.mil/doctrine and Joint Doctrine Education and Training Electronic Information System https://jdeis.js.mil/jdeis/index.jsp. Also located on SECRET Internet Protocol Router Network (SIPRNET) at http://nmcc20a.nmcc.smil/mil/dj9j7ead/doctrine. The Joint Electronic Library is the primary site for current and draft JPs.

b. Defense Link Home page: http://www.defenselink.mil. Defense Link is an entry point for Internet sites for Services, Secretary of Defense, and related agencies. Includes information about combatant commands and selected PO.

c. NGA: http://www.nga.mil. Also located on SIPRNET at http://www.nga.smil.mil.

d. Center for Defense Information Home page: http://www.cdi.org. Publishes a bi-weekly listing recent publications on peacekeeping and multilateral military operations.

e. UNDPKO Home page: http://www.un.org/Depts/dpko/dpko/index.asp.

f. United States Institute of Peace: http://www.usip.org. This site contains information by and about the United States Institute of Peace and a collection of links to Internet resources relating to international conflict resolution, negotiation theory, and peace studies.

g. US DOS Office of the Coordinator for Reconstruction and Stabilization: http://www.state.gov/s/crs.

APPENDIX D
ADMINISTRATIVE INSTRUCTIONS

1. User Comments

Users in the field are highly encouraged to submit comments on this publication to: Commander, United States Joint Forces Command, Joint Warfighting Center, ATTN: Doctrine Group, 116 Lake View Parkway, Suffolk, VA 23435-2697. These comments should address content (accuracy, usefulness, consistency, and organization), writing, and appearance.

2. Authorship

The lead agent for this publication is the US Army. The Joint Staff doctrine sponsor for this publication is the Director for Strategic Plans and Policy (J-5).

3. Supersession

This publication supersedes JP 3-07.3, 12 February 1999, *Joint Tactics, Techniques, and Procedures for Peace Operations.*

4. Change Recommendations

a. Recommendations for urgent changes to this publication should be submitted:

```
TO:     DA WASHINGTON DC//G35-SSP//
INFO:   JOINT STAFF WASHINGTON DC//J7-JEDD//
        CDRUSJFCOM SUFFOLK VA//DJT10//
```

Routine changes should be submitted electronically to Commander, Joint Warfighting Center, Joint Doctrine Group and info the Lead Agent and the Director for Operational Plans and Joint Force Development J-7/JEDD via the CJCS JEL at http://www.dtic.mil/doctrine.

b. When a Joint Staff directorate submits a proposal to the Chairman of the Joint Chiefs of Staff that would change source document information reflected in this publication, that directorate will include a proposed change to this publication as an enclosure to its proposal. The Military Services and other organizations are requested to notify the Joint Staff J-7 when changes to source documents reflected in this publication are initiated.

c. Record of Changes:

CHANGE NUMBER	COPY NUMBER	DATE OF CHANGE	DATE ENTERED	POSTED BY	REMARKS

5. Distribution of Publications

Local reproduction is authorized and access to unclassified publications is unrestricted. However, access to and reproduction authorization for classified joint publications must be in accordance with DOD Regulation 5200.1-R, *Information Security Program*.

6. Distribution of Electronic Publications

a. Joint Staff J-7 will not print copies of JPs for distribution. Electronic versions are available on JDEIS at https://jdeis.js.mil (NIPRNET), and https://jdeis.js.smil.mil (SIPRNET) and on the JEL at http://www.dtic.mil/doctrine (NIPRNET).

b. Only approved joint publications and joint test publications are releasable outside the combatant commands, Services, and Joint Staff. Release of any classified joint publication to foreign governments or foreign nationals must be requested through the local embassy (Defense Attaché Office) to DIA Foreign Liaison Office, PO-FL, Room 1E811, 7400 Pentagon, Washington, DC 20301-7400.

c. CD-ROM. Upon request of a JDDC member, the Joint Staff J-7 will produce and deliver one CD-ROM with current joint publications.

GLOSSARY
PART I — ABBREVIATIONS AND ACRONYMS

AFCAP	Air Force contract augmentation program
AFTTP(I)	Air Force tactics, techniques, and procedures (instruction)
AJP	Allied joint publication
BZ	buffer zone
C2	command and control
CA	civil affairs
CAO	civil affairs operations
CBRN	chemical, biological, radiological, and nuclear
CCDR	combatant commander
CIMIC	civil-military cooperation
CIVPOL	civilian police
CJCS	Chairman of the Joint Chiefs of Staff
CJCSI	Chairman of the Joint Chiefs of Staff instruction
CMO	civil-military operations
CMOC	civil-military operations center
CONOPS	concept of operations
CSS	combat service support
DC	dislocated civilian
DDRRR	disarmament, demobilization, repatriation, reintegration, and resettlement
DMZ	demilitarized zone
DOD	Department of Defense
DODD	Department of Defense directive
DOJ	Department of Justice
DOS	Department of State
DPKO	Department of Peacekeeping Operations
EOD	explosive ordnance disposal
EU	European Union
FAO	Food and Agriculture Organization (UN)
FHA	foreign humanitarian assistance
FM	field manual (Army)
FP	force protection
GCC	geographic combatant commander
GEOINT	geospatial intelligence

HA	humanitarian assistance
HAZMAT	hazardous materials
HN	host nation
HNS	host-nation support
HOM	head of mission
HSS	health service support
HUMINT	human intelligence
IGO	intergovernmental organization
IO	information operations
IPI	indigenous populations and institutions
I/R	internment/resettlement
JFC	joint force commander
JP	joint publication
JTF	joint task force
LNO	liaison officer
LOGCAP	logistics civil augmentation program
MCWP	Marine Corps warfighting publication
MILOB	military observer
MNF	multinational force
MNFC	multinational force commander
MOE	measure of effectiveness
MOU	memorandum of understanding
MP	military police (Army and Marine)
NATO	North Atlantic Treaty Organization
NGA	National Geospatial-Intelligence Agency
NGO	nongovernmental organization
OAS	Organization of American States
OAU	Organization of African Unity
OCHA	Office for the Coordination of Humanitarian Affairs
OGA	other government agency
OMS	Office of Mission Support
OPCON	operational control
PA	public affairs
PB	peace building
PEO	peace enforcement operations
PKO	peacekeeping operations
PM	peacemaking
PO	peace operations

PSO	peace support operations (NATO)
PSYOP	psychological operations
R&R	rest and recuperation
ROE	rules of engagement
SECARMY	Secretary of the Army
SF	security force
SIPRNET	SECRET Internet Protocol Router Network
SOF	special operations forces
SOFA	status-of-forces agreement
SOMA	status of mission agreement
SOP	standing operating procedure
SRSG	special representative of the Secretary-General
TOR	term of reference
UN	United Nations
UN-DMT	United Nations disaster management team
UNDP	United Nations development programme
UNDPKO	United Nations Department for Peacekeeping Operations
UNHCR	United Nations Office of the High Commissioner for Refugees
UNICEF	United Nations Children's Fund
UNSC	United Nations Security Council
UNSCR	United Nations Security Council resolution
UNSG	United Nations Secretary-General
USAID	United States Agency for International Development
USCG	United States Coast Guard
USG	United States Government
USMOG-W	United States Military Observer Group — Washington
USYG	Under Secretary General
WFP	World Food Programme (UN)
WHO	World Health Organization (UN)
WMD	weapons of mass destruction

Unless otherwise annotated, this publication is the proponent for all terms and definitions found in the glossary. Upon approval, JP 1-02 will reflect this publication as the source document for these terms and definitions.

area of limitation. A defined area where specific limitations apply to the strength and fortifications of disputing or belligerent forces. Normally, upper limits are established for the number and type of formations, tanks, antiaircraft weapons, artillery, and other weapons systems in the area of limitation. Also called AOL. (JP 3-07.3)

area of separation. See buffer zone. Also called AOS. (JP 3-07.3)

armistice. In international law, a suspension or temporary cessation of hostilities by agreement between belligerent powers. (JP 3-07.3)

armistice demarcation line. A geographically defined line from which disputing or belligerent forces disengage and withdraw to their respective sides following a truce or cease fire agreement. Also called cease fire line in some United Nations operations. Also called ADL. (JP 3-07.3)

buffer zone. 1. A defined area controlled by a peace operations force from which disputing or belligerent forces have been excluded. A buffer zone is formed to create an area of separation between disputing or belligerent forces and reduce the risk of renewed conflict. Also called area of separation in some United Nations operations. Also called BZ. (JP 3-07.3)

cease fire line. See armistice demarcation line. (JP 3-07.3)

civil affairs operations. Those military operations conducted by civil affairs forces that (1) enhance the relationship between military forces and civil authorities in localities where military forces are present; (2) require coordination with other interagency organizations, intergovernmental organizations, nongovernmental organizations, indigenous population and institutions, and the private sector; and (3) involve application of functional specialty skills that normally are the responsibility of civil government to enhance the conduct of civil-military operations. Also called CAO. (This term and its definition are provided for information and are proposed for inclusion in JP 1-02 by JP 3-57.)

conflict prevention. A peace operation employing complementary diplomatic, civil, and, when necessary, military means, to monitor and identify the causes of conflict, and take timely action to prevent the occurrence, escalation, or resumption of hostilities. Activities aimed at conflict prevention are often conducted under Chapter VI of the United Nations Charter. Conflict prevention can include fact-finding missions, consultations, warnings, inspections, and monitoring. (Approved for inclusion in the next edition of JP 1-02.)

demilitarized zone. A defined area in which the stationing or concentrating of military forces, or the retention or establishment of military installations of any description, is prohibited. (JP 3-07.3)

dislocated civilian. A broad term that includes a displaced person, an evacuee, an expellee, an internally displaced person, a migrant, a refugee, or a stateless person. Also called DC. (JP 3-57.1)

line of demarcation. A line defining the boundary of a buffer zone or area of limitation. A line of demarcation may also be used to define the forward limits of disputing or belligerent forces after each phase of disengagement or withdrawal has been completed. (JP 3-07.3)

nation assistance. Civil and/or military assistance rendered to a nation by foreign forces within that nation's territory during peacetime, crises or emergencies, or war based on agreements mutually concluded between nations. Nation assistance programs include, but are not limited to, security assistance, foreign internal defense, other Title 10, US Code programs, and activities performed on a reimbursable basis by Federal agencies or intergovernmental organizations. (JP 3-0)

operations to restore order. Operations intended to halt violence and support, reinstate, or establish civil authorities. They are designed to return an unstable and lawless environment to the point where indigenous police forces can effectively enforce the law and restore civil authority. (JP 3-07.3)

peace building. Stability actions, predominately diplomatic and economic, that strengthen and rebuild governmental infrastructure and institutions in order to avoid a relapse into conflict. Also called PB. (JP 3-0)

peace enforcement. Application of military force or the threat of its use, normally pursuant to international authorization, to compel compliance with resolutions or sanctions designed to maintain or restore peace and order. (JP 3-0)

peacekeeping. Military operations undertaken with the consent of all major parties to a dispute, designed to monitor and facilitate implementation of an agreement (cease fire, truce, or other such agreement) and support diplomatic efforts to reach a long-term political settlement. (This term and its definition modify the existing term and its definition and are approved for inclusion in the next edition of JP 1-02.)

peacemaking. The process of diplomacy, mediation, negotiation, or other forms of peaceful settlements that arranges an end to a dispute and resolves issues that led to it. (JP 3-0)

peace operations. A broad term that encompasses multiagency and multinational crisis response and limited contingency operations involving all instruments of national power with military missions to contain conflict, redress the peace, and shape the environment to support reconciliation and rebuilding and facilitate the transition to legitimate governance. Peace operations include peacekeeping, peace enforcement, peacemaking, peace building, and conflict prevention efforts. Also called PO.

(This term and its definition modify the existing term and its definition and are approved for inclusion in the next edition of JP 1-02.)

preventive deployment. The deployment of military forces to deter violence at the interface or zone of potential conflict where tension is rising among parties. Forces may be employed in such a way that they are indistinguishable from a peace operations force in terms of equipment, force posture, and activities. (This term and its definition modify the existing term and its definition and are approved for inclusion in the next edition of JP 1-02.)

public diplomacy. 1. Those overt international public information activities of the United States Government designed to promote United States foreign policy objectives by seeking to understand, inform, and influence foreign audiences and opinion makers, and by broadening the dialogue between American citizens and institutions and their counterparts abroad. 2. In peace building, civilian agency efforts to promote an understanding of the reconstruction efforts, rule of law, and civic responsibility through public affairs and international public diplomacy operations. Its objective is to promote and sustain consent for peace building both within the host nation and externally in the region and in the larger international community. (This term and its definition modify the existing term and its definition and are approved for inclusion in the next edition of JP 1-02.)

JOINT DOCTRINE PUBLICATIONS HIERARCHY

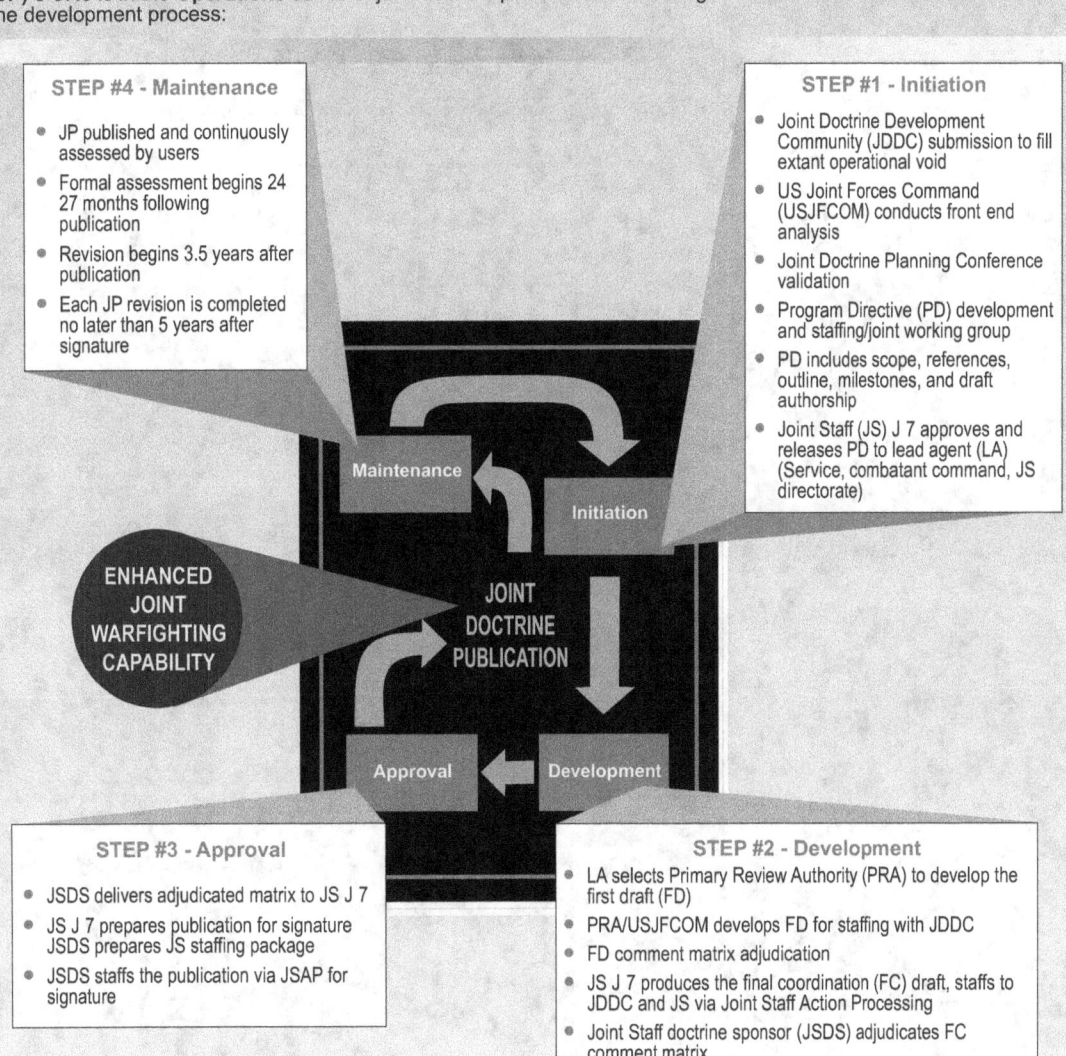

All joint publications are organized into a comprehensive hierarchy as shown in the chart above. **Joint Publication (JP) 3-07.3** is in the **Operations** series of joint doctrine publications. The diagram below illustrates an overview of the development process:

STEP #4 - Maintenance

- JP published and continuously assessed by users
- Formal assessment begins 24 27 months following publication
- Revision begins 3.5 years after publication
- Each JP revision is completed no later than 5 years after signature

STEP #1 - Initiation

- Joint Doctrine Development Community (JDDC) submission to fill extant operational void
- US Joint Forces Command (USJFCOM) conducts front end analysis
- Joint Doctrine Planning Conference validation
- Program Directive (PD) development and staffing/joint working group
- PD includes scope, references, outline, milestones, and draft authorship
- Joint Staff (JS) J 7 approves and releases PD to lead agent (LA) (Service, combatant command, JS directorate)

STEP #3 - Approval

- JSDS delivers adjudicated matrix to JS J 7
- JS J 7 prepares publication for signature JSDS prepares JS staffing package
- JSDS staffs the publication via JSAP for signature

STEP #2 - Development

- LA selects Primary Review Authority (PRA) to develop the first draft (FD)
- PRA/USJFCOM develops FD for staffing with JDDC
- FD comment matrix adjudication
- JS J 7 produces the final coordination (FC) draft, staffs to JDDC and JS via Joint Staff Action Processing
- Joint Staff doctrine sponsor (JSDS) adjudicates FC comment matrix
- FC Joint working group